Aside from being an informative piece of literature offering insight into the grandest scheme the world has ever known, this book is a drinking game. Take a sip of your favorite alcoholic beverage each time a pop culture reference is made.

Drink Responsibly.

"Steady."
"I'm steady."
"Relax."
"I'm relaxed!"
"Relax."
Sighs. "Turn on the music."
"Uh...What switch?"
"I don't know what half of 'em do. Try that one."
He flips it on, and Johnny Cash's 'Ring of Fire' is
playing.
"Turn it up."
He presses the button next to it a few times. They both
bob their heads a bit. And tap their feet.
"Good song."
"Real good song."
"You see that movie. Uh…"
"Walk the Line!"
"Joaquin Phoenix. Excellent job."
"Not bad. Not bad. Not as good as--"
"Robbed at the Oscars."
"--the nigger who played Ray Charles."
"Uh...Jamie..."
"Foxx."
"Phenomenal job."
"Oh, he was *Ray Charles."*
"No doubt."
"Talented nigger."
"Both, very talented niggers."
"Altitude!"
"Ok!"
"You see it?"
"I see it."
"You see that poosy, too, eh?"
"Yeah. Smell it too." They laugh.

"I don't think either of those movies has been filmed yet."

Opening the door to the cockpit and poking his head in is Leslie Nielson from the 1980 movie **Airplane!**: "I just want to tell you both good luck. We're all counting on you." And he shuts the door.

"I'm going to kill him." He pulls out the box cutter.

"Put that thing away. You want to hurt somebody?"

"He does it one more time. I swear."

"I'm trying to fly a plane!"

"Oh, here it comes."

"Praise Allah."

"Praise Allah."

In unison: "Poosy Heaven!"

Down below on the streets of Manhattan, someone hollers: "Oh shit!"

The plane crashes into the side of the north tower of the World Trade Center.

The two hijackers meet up with the other three from the rear of the plane, on a wide open prairie. It's strewn with hundreds of slaughtered sheep. Pieces of wool cloud the air. In the center of it is a large wooden cross sticking out of the ground. The top of it is scorched and the two metal spikes on either end of the horizontal board have raw bloody meat hanging off of them.

"This is poosy heaven?"

Behind the five men emerges the shadow of the rising sun, its rays swaying side to side rhythmically to a primitive drumbeat.

Pop Illuminati
Volume I:
The New World Order Conspiracy
and
Popular Culture

Randy Cunningham

DYNATOX MINISTRIES

Borneo – East Brunswick – Reseda

For Krall

"I am a most unhappy man. I have unwittingly ruined my country. A great industrial nation is controlled by its system of credit. Our system of credit is concentrated. The growth of the nation, therefore, and all our activities are in the hands of a few men. We have come to be one of the worst ruled, one of the most completely controlled and dominated governments in the civilized world. No longer a government by free opinion, no longer a government by conviction and the vote of the majority, but a government by the opinion and duress of a small group of dominant men."
~President Woodrow Wilson: 1916

"Some...ideological extremists at either end of the political spectrum....believe we are part of a secret cabal working against the best interests of the United States, characterizing my family and me as "internationalists" and of conspiring with others around the world to build a more integrated global political and economic structure—one world, if you will. If that's the charge, I stand guilty, and I am proud of it."
~ David Rockefeller: Memoirs, Chapter 27 – Proud Internationalist, page 405; Random House; 2002.

"All propaganda has to be popular and has to adapt its spiritual level to the perception of the least intelligent of those towards whom it intends to direct itself."
~ Adolph Hitler, *Mein Kampf,* translated by Ralph Manheim. Boston: Houghton Mifflin Company, 1943.

"I have come here to kick ass and chew bubblegum …And I'm all out of bubblegum."
~Roddy Piper in *They Live* (Dir: John Carpenter, 1988)

John Carpenter's cult film *They Live* is about a race of extraterrestrial beings set to enslave the human race. Its protagonist, played by former WWF wrestler "Rowdy" Roddy Piper, has stumbled upon their secret agenda. Having acquired a pair of special sunglasses, he can see the infiltrators' real alien appearances behind their humanoid façades. And that's not all he sees—the sunglasses decipher subliminal messages meant for reception by the masses of unsuspecting earthlings. Sporting his Ray-Bans, Piper looks on in astonishment as a billboard ad for a tropical vacation becomes the command: "Marry and Reproduce." Other public signs, magazine ads, etc, reveal hidden messages such as: "Consume", "Obey", "Watch TV", "Stay Asleep", "No Thought", "Do Not Question Authority", "No Imagination", "Conform", etc.

Roddy's view of the world is flipped upside down. He tries to recruit friends to join the cause of defeating the aliens and saving the world from tyranny but nobody wants to listen to his bullshit. In one of the movie's best scenes, Piper gets into a back alley brawl complete with body slams and other wrestling moves that drags on forever. All he's attempting to do is convince his friend to try on the specs and see the truth of their situation for himself. The scene is a powerful metaphor for the resistance we awakened folk face every time we attempt to present evidence on the New World Order conspiracy to people unfamiliar with it.

They Live is a fictionalized imagining of a real life conspiracy involving a secret society whose objective is to depopulate the earth of most of its people as it establishes a one-world totalitarian government, commonly referred to as the New World Order (NWO). The secret society is called the Illuminati. Its top dogs are in the highest positions in government, academia, business, entertainment, and media the world over. The 911 "terrorist" attacks were a crucial plot point in this conspiracy, acting as the catalyst to streamline the New World Order. The faltering economy is likewise guiding us that direction. As a sovereign nation and a planet of 8 billion people, we are nearing the end. It is a matter of years, months, weeks, days before cataclysm strikes our current world order. Whether there is an extraterrestrial origin to this conspiracy--as in Carpenter's *They Live*-- is debated about as much as whether there's a satanic or biblical origin. Or a human origin. Or…..so on, around the world twice, and back again through infinity and beyond.

They Live is an obvious example of the Illuminati revealing their conspiracy to us in the guise of entertainment. For other examples, often more subtle, take your pick of any modern Hollywood movie, or any popular song on your radio, or watch any sitcom, action show, reality series, talk show, news show, on all mainstream networks: CBS, FOX, ABC, NBC, Comedy Central, TNT, TBS, SPIKE, THE HALMARK CHANNEL, TBN, PBS. Just turn on the fucking television set.

They reveal their dominance and their secret agenda to us subconsciously. They condition our living patterns and habits. They create our cultural and subcultural norms (e.g., 'Here's how a Midwestern hick family should behave--tune into *Rosanne*.'). They manipulate us into thinking and behaving in specific ways in given situations ('here's how you handle an embarrassing situation such as that, watch *Seinfeld*.'). They mislead and lie to us—the mainstream media and our government collaborating to deceive us. The political circus with its dunce cast of characters portraying womanizers, incompetents, swindlers, and closet Muslims duking it out, while we the public take sides, is as real as professional wrestling. They've been doing this since the beginning of American television. Your parents fell for it. You've fallen for it. You're teaching your children to fall for it.

And the programming is getting more insidious and ominous in recent years. More so than ever before in America, mysterious and cryptic images flood our minds via the media and the world of entertainment and popular culture. Bizarre symbols of pyramids, all-seeing-eyes, rising suns, eclipses and pentagrams dance about the edge of our conscious awareness. Public photos of our recent Presidents show them and their families flashing satanic hand gestures, such as devil horns, at us. There's fanatical America worship rivaling the degree of nationalism displayed in Nazi Germany. Toxic chemical streams (chemtrails) murk up our once clear blue skies, and we pay no mind. Our rights are progressively stolen from us by all areas of the political spectrum, and we turn the other cheek. This has all been accompanied by an upsurge in the conspiracy theory industry--in the form of books, alternative media shows, documentaries, Youtube videos, websites, lectures, and the rap music scene.

People say, "Show me proof!" My response: Where are you looking? The proof is everywhere staring you in the face. The Illuminati are being so obvious now that they appear to be making their omnipresence and NWO conspiracy known to us on a *conscious* level. As the dawn of the New World Order approaches--and for reasons we'll get into--they're stirring a bunch of us awake.

The weapon they are welding to control and awaken us is the world we're all familiar with. Collectively it is our movies, TV programs, popular music, games, internet connection, consumer goods, and our public domain. It's Facebook. It's Youtube. It's our malls. Our clothes, our tastes, our shallow views. It's what's in style. Our celebrity worship and electronics fetishes. Our interpersonal interactions. Fast food. It's consumerism. Propaganda. Our values, thoughts, opinions, and beliefs. And our personal styles and public personas. Singularly it is a manufactured reality. A hologram. A matrix. A script. A secret game. A program. To program you and me and societies to behave in accordance with the hidden (in plain sight) New World Order agenda. It is popular culture and may fittingly be called Pop Illuminati.

"There are no experts."
~Father Damien Karras in *The Exorcist* (Directed by William Friedkin, 1973)

I call myself and others like me *awake*. It essentially means that we are aware of the New World Order conspiracy. Understand, if you try to change our minds, it won't happen. We are convinced of what we claim we know as truth. We have our individual theories in regards to details, methods, origin, etc. So, we don't know it all (only the Illuminated at the top of the pyramid knows it all), even though most of us think we do.

This book is for the awakened and the non-awakened. I'll start with a general overview of the Illuminati and New World Order conspiracy theory. Once we're all up to speed, we'll venture into the world of Pop Illuminati. In a nutshell, I will provide you a snapshot of the hellish, Orwellian nightmare you currently live in. For you to see it. And then crumple up as your conditioned mind tells you to do. Or perhaps you'll see your situation for how it is.

We'll look at some of the more pertinent, popular, blatant and interesting instances of Pop Illuminati. There are literally too many instances to consider them all here. Youtube is a fun place to obtain a lot of very useful information. I still encourage you to locate primary sources whenever the clip you are watching is not the primary source, for there is much deceptive information (disinformation) to be found on Youtube, and a lot of garbage (which can be fun, too).

I offer more in this writing than a mere survey of alleged examples and existing theories within theories. You'll be able to locate quite a bit surfing Youtube, yourselves. Generally, when I do mention known theories or examples, I elaborate only when I have my own insights, spins, or interpretations that I wish to share. In short, my own ideas and observations—my own theories—are what I'm most interested in leaving with you. Yet, I am not so foolish to believe that my ideas developed in a vacuum deep within my groovy, grey nugget.

Other than a strict no-bubblegum policy, I keep things pretty loose here. Disagree all you want. Also, I'm not here to bust out any one person. There's no mind-blowing proof of anything in these pages. This is entertainment. Like anything else, it's Pop Illuminati.

Pop Illuminati Challenge! What Nirvana CD, released before September 11ᵗʰ, 2001, provides a clue of the impending 911 "terrorist" attacks, on its inner sleeve when examined through a mirror?

(Answers to the Pop Illuminati Challenge! feature of this game are not included in these pages.)

"*Mom!*"

"*What?!*"

"*He's back!*"

"*Where?*" Sighing.

"*Behind the door!*"

Of course there's no one behind my bedroom door.

She laughs.

"*Don't laugh!*" *Still crying.*

"*I'm sorry, whiny. It's just…foolish. There's no…pointy-head man.*"

"*The pointy-head man!*"

She shouldn't have said the name. Now he'll never shut up. And she'll never sleep.

Now I see him. It had only been the shadowy triangular face with the single glowing eyeball above the beak-like nose. He ducked behind the door when mom burst in flipping on the light. But I see him in my mind. He's tall, spindly. His skull is a freakish marvel, encased in pale wrinkled skin. He starts tearing up my room. Why does he tear up my room? Seething. Cracked lips snarling. Bulging navy blue eye enraged, darting over periodically, dark brow twitching frenetically. Berserk! Hitting the walls, sweat slopping off the slanted four-sided head. And then he stops and turns quiet. He walks briskly over to my bedside, hunkers down and I scream.

Somewhere beyond the swirl, mom chuckles her concern.

The Illuminati and the New World Order Conspiracy

"Pull the strings! Pull the strings!"
~Bela Lugosi in *Glen or Glenda* (Directed by Edward D. Wood, Jr., 1953)

Not everyone who is awake to the New World Order conspiracy believes the Illuminati is behind it. It's plausible that the Illuminati does not really exist and an equally powerful Illuminati-like group 'pulls the strings.' You'll often hear popular conspiracy theorists offer a broader name--usually one with less mystique. The NWO conspirators are sometimes called the globalists, the power elite, the elite, the wealthy one percent, or simply the New World Order, among many other synonyms. The name however is inconsequential if the agenda is identical with the original Illuminati's. Thus, through-out this book I shall continue referring to New World Order conspirators as the Illuminati.

The Order of the Illuminati, established on May 1st, 1776 (familiar sounding year?) has its roots in 15th century Europe in such secret orders as the Freemasons and the Rosicrucians. Wait, let's go back further and discuss the influence of Egyptian gods, astrology, and witchcraft. But shit, that superstitious mumbo jumbo was likely started by whoever was responsible for creating the earth and placing that fake moon up in the sky. Maybe it's The Grand Architect of the Universe that the Masons refer to? Whoever the fuck *that* is....It does not matter, however, as the Order of the Illuminati disbanded in 1785. Whew. Close one. Good thing.

"You didn't think I was *dead*....did you?"
~**Anthony Perkins as Dr. Jekyll and Mr. Hyde/Jack the Ripper in *Edge of Sanity* (Directed by Gérard Kikoíne, 1989)**

Anyway...the Illuminati is hell-bent on bringing chaos and destruction to the current world system in order to usher in the New World Order. They are behind our impending world economic collapse, as inflation (never mind the deceptive consumer price index, which doesn't even take into account the rising costs of power and food) and unemployment continue to increase. They have engineered all the major health crises in our modern world--heart disease, high blood pressure, high cholesterol, diabetes, depression, social anxiety, panic disorder, GERD, Gout, Alzheimer's, autism, HIV, cancer, flu, and all other life threatening diseases that bring rich white bastards large profit margins. They were behind the 911 'terrorist' attacks and blamed it on Muslim extremists as certainly as the Bush Jr. administration lied about weapons of mass destruction in Iraq. Hundreds of thousands of misguided people are being killed or tortured or driven mad and to suicide daily in these Illuminati-generated wars. War is big business. The Illuminati owns the world leaders waging the wars. They pull the strings on all sides. And why not treat the troops fighting on all sides--the insurgents, the U.S. military, what have you-- as if they are *RISK* game pieces? U.S. citizens are disposable resources. Used for the sole purpose of bringing about the New World Order.

The structure of the Illuminati is a hierarchical pyramid. At the apex of the pyramid is the all-seeing-eye, representing the supreme leader(s) of this secret society. This representation is most popularly (and fittingly) depicted on the U.S. dollar bill. As the pyramid descends, there are a greater number of Illuminati members at each successive level. The lower the level of the pyramid a member is located, the less power he or she commands and, subsequently, the less knowledge of the operation as a whole he or she possesses. Folks near the bottom of the pyramid, for instance, might understand that they are involved in something shady, and get paid well for it, but might not know the malevolent force behind it. Or they have an idea of a malevolent force and just don't care--after all, they're getting paid and their family is allowed to live.

The lust for greed and power surges through it all and is its lifeblood. The pyramid is composed of business people, CEOs, politicians, public officials, military personnel, actors and actresses (both B and A grade), movie and television producers and directors, TV talk show hosts, news correspondents, clergy, historians, physics professors, mathematicians, engineers, biochemists, university deans, world leaders, popular conspiracy theorists, the Freemasons (the organization of the Freemasons itself a secret society with a pyramidal structure and used as a recruitment and promotion tool by the illuminati).

Who's at the top? Whose Eye is it? The Masons will tell you the Eye represents *God* (the lower degree ones actually believing this claim). On the other hand, it would not surprise me if a large portion of the U.S. population doesn't even know there is a pyramid on the dollar bill.

Depending on the theorist, the true 'Eye-dentity,' if you will humor me, ranges from Satan (or Lucifer), an interdimensional reptilian shapeshifting alien race (made most popular by pioneering conspiracy theorist/writer/lecturer David Icke), the United Nations, the Rothschilds, the Zionists, the British Royalty, the Federal Reserve, the Vatican, to the Egyptian sun god Horus or Ra, Shiva the Hindu God of Destruction, and Saturn (not nearly an exhaustive list) or some combination of all these.

Is the Eye really 'all-seeing'? How far into your minds and lives has the Eye penetrated, using the information to manipulate and control you—shaping your preferences, opinions, most cherished and fundamental beliefs, your behavior, your personality? Without a doubt, as technology advances, how deeply the Eye sees into your life increases. We know about tracking devices on cars and iPhones, warrantless wiretapping via The Patriot Act, satellite surveillance, drones, and we regularly engage in online personal information input and financial transactions.

If the NWO conspiracy is true, it is technologically and theoretically plausible and very likely that cell phones, personal computers, television sets…all electronics …currently have hidden cameras and audio recording devices installed into them. Running. Now. The Illuminati has the resources, capabilities, means, and motive. If you've ever read Orwell's *1984* you were probably thinking at the time: *Man, that would suck to have a telescreen watching you every day, all day, in public and in private.* At the very least, in that novel the public was made aware that they were continuously monitored and recorded by their tyrannical government. I don't know which way is worse-- knowing or not knowing. In Pop Illuminati most of us get to bask in the delusion of privacy. For now. The wise Illuminati owl understands,

I'm presuming, the value of information obtained via observation of people who don't know they are being watched. It makes sense that they would want to establish a baseline to compare with our behavior once we know we are being watched.

In the course of this drinking game, you might have said to yourself, "There's a lot of intelligent, well-informed people in the U.S.A. If any of this conspiracy crap were true, they'd have figured it out." No, there's not. There are a lot of intelligent *but brainwashed* people. The ones who see it and speak up are marginalized, persecuted, corrupted, or silenced.

To expand your NWO conspiracy theory literacy, I've put together a list (in no particular order) of topics and names frequently associated with the New World Order conspiracy theory. Just keyword any of these phrases either by itself or with 'Illuminati' or 'New World Order' on Google or Youtube for access to a wealth of information, misinformation, and disinformation.

Chemtrails
United Nations
911 False Flag
911 Inside Job
Psyops
Propaganda
Brainwashing
Internment Camps
Totalitarian Government
RFID Chips
Fluoride in water
HAARP Program
Orwellian
911 Truth Movement
Antichrist
Apocalypse
Vaccines
Autism
Deliberate Dumbing Down of America
Freemasons
33rd Degree Freemason
All-Seeing-Eye
Eye of Ra
Eye of Horus
Pentagrams
Hexagrams

Pyramid
Sun
Rising Sun
Stars
Sun gods
Saturn
Nibiru
Planet X
Shill
Disinformation Agent
Satan
Lucifer
Baphomet
Molech
Goat of Mendez
Pan
Ra
Horus
Astrology
Sacred geometry
Reptilians
Kabbalah
witchcraft
black magic
Illuminati Symbology
Illuminati Symbolism
Shadow Government
Military Industrial Complex
The Patriot Act
National Defense Authorization Act
World Trade Center Building 7
"Two Planes, Three Towers"
David Icke
Alex Jones

Jesse Ventura
Ron Paul
Jordan Maxwell
Controlled Demolition
North American Union
United Corporation of America
European Union
The Federal Reserve
Rothschild
Rockefeller
Secret Societies
Skull and Bones
Knights Templar
Bohemian Grove
European Union
Fiat Money
The Bilderberg Group
The Council on Foreign Relations
The Trilateral Commission
Surveillance
Tyranny
Martial Law
Police State
Department of Homeland Security
Loose Change Documentary
Domestic Terrorism
The Georgia Guidestones
Denver International Airport
Geological Warfare
Biochemical Warfare
Thermite
"Rainman" Rap Music
Ritual abuse
Gulf of Tonkin

JFK Assassination
False American History
Masonic architecture in D.C.
Ritual Sacrifice
Illuminati and Freemason hand signs and handshakes.
Predictive Programming
Checkpoints
Drones
Warrantless Wiretapping
CISPA
Military Industrial Complex
Occupy Wall Street
IRS
Al Quaida
Hitler
Prescott Bush
Prince William
Bloodlines
Bill of Rights
Brainwashing
Information War
Zionists
British Royalty
subliminal messaging
Holy Bible
Gnosticism
Theosophy
Stanley P. Hall
Madam Blavatsky
Luciferianism
Book of Genesis
Bill Cooper
Ancient Alien/Astronaut theories
Christian Theology

The Book of Revelation
UFOlogy
Alien Abductions
Maitreya
Tree of Knowledge
Gulf of Tonkin
Sociopaths
Bush
Obama
The Occult
MK Ultra
Economic Collapse
Hyperinflation
Unemployment
Consumerism
Corporatism
Banker Ponzi Scheme
International Monetary Fund
World Bank
War games morning of 911
JFK Assassination
Abraham Lincoln Assassination
Illusion of Freedom
George Carlin
Bill Hicks
Communism
Socialism
Fascism
Capitalism
Democracy
Republic
The Constitution
Thought Police
CIA

Osama Bin Laden
War on Terror
The 911 Commission
Carbon Taxes
Global Warming
FEMA
FEMA Coffins (liners)
FEMA Camps
FEMA fusion centers
Class Warfare
Big Brother
Gun Ban/Control
TARP
911 First Responders Illness

Pop Illuminati Challenge! Chant "Yes We Can" into a recording device. Play it in reverse. Are you now chanting, "Thank You Satan!"?

Pop Illuminati

Becoming aware of the Illuminati and its agenda is the most shocking, infuriating, frightening, thrilling, intriguing, and entertaining development that's ever happened to me. As I and kindred 'see-ers' attend to events, advertisements and entertainments around us we notice patterns, connect "the dots", and attempt to decipher symbols and other hidden meaning associated with the New World Order. And believe you me, they're there. All the time. Everywhere. It's on the radio (e.g., Madonna, Tupac, all pop music) and on TV (from *Spongebob Square Pants* to the *NBC Nightly News*), the silver screen (we've all seen *Ghostbusters*, and any other Hollywood movie), internet pages (ads upon ads of brand logos containing Illuminati symbolism), on billboards (that's a huge motherfucking eye!), in magazines (many people still read these). We receive a message…sporting Piper's special sun glasses…only our lenses are a bit warped, accounting for variance among the awakened's interpretation of the message, inciting more conflict and drama. Intrigue. We who are awake see the rope connected to the bucket in Brian De Palma's *Carrie* (1976). We know the vileness the bucket contains and that it is about to be tipped. We're drawn in, deeper….deeper. It's exciting. Everything has the mark of the Illuminati brand. Watch any national TV commercial, show, or movie—if you put on Roddy's Raybans, i.e. pay attention, you'll find it.

"You're traveling through another dimension..."
~ **Rod Serling, opening to** *The Twilight Zone* **(1959-1964)**

The Illuminati has the mass media set up so that everyone behaves as though nothing is the matter. War is mentioned in a news story briefly and then it's onto a celebrity break up story or your latest mother-killing-child case update, followed by the evening cognitive-behavioral programming--portraying fictional characters (yes even the ones in so-called reality TV shows) as though they are real people that we should identify with.

Depending on the show, the characters look like our family. They behave like us, engage in the same mundane tasks. They laugh. They cry. They have a ball. They communicate to their spouse in this manner. They discipline their children in that that way. They strive to be grateful for their close-quartered enslavement.

Perhaps you live a working class life in a Midwestern rural town, you may make room for the occasional *Rosanne* rerun (as I guiltily do). Watching the Connors struggle, have fights, work like slaves but still have loads of fun and blessed lives, you subconsciously find yourself viewing your own enslaved life as a blessing. Not only do you identify with the characters, you pick up their habits, traits, mannerisms, and opinions. You learn the 'socially appropriate' behavior of that demographic. Maybe you're of the 'hip' variety, gravitating toward repeats of *Friends* and learning fun and vibrant ways to interact with your own friends. If you are a conspiracy theorist, you pick up (potentially destructive) ways to refute anti-conspiracy theorist claims by modeling Alex Jones. In short, we model the behavior of the characters we watch, and we model each other modeling the behavior.

Pop Illuminati Challenge! Reflect on the TV Shows you watch. Do you see how you attempt to identify with or emulate the characters? Pay attention to your own thinking, speaking and actions in your daily life and compare them with those of the characters in your TV (or movie) programming. Pay attention also to when you model behaviors of people you know.

The Illuminati has a love affair with symbols. All big corporations incorporate Illuminati symbolism into their logo designs. You'll see three Illuminati symbols more than any of the others: the all-seeing-eye, the pyramid (often with some bright light source emanating about the apex), and the sun (often rising; also sun rays). Other very common symbols are: the earth or globe (more so lately I've noticed), Saturn (or the rings of Saturn, such as in the Bud light logo and Nike swoosh and that ring around the *e* on your Internet explorer icon), stars (inverted pentagrams), hexagrams (the star of David), yin yang type symbols, the number 6 (or 666), a serpent (often a snake in a circle, or two winding up a cross) a bird wingspread, an eclipse, a torch, a crown, a ladder (could represent both the Mason's ladder and Jacob's Ladder), a Masonic compass, black and white pattern (like a chessboard) and crossed lines (like an 'X'-- look at your Microsoft Windows logo for an illustration).

Even when there is not a recognizably identifiable sun symbol, many of these logos are designed with an unseen point of light radiating from 'behind' the logo, suggesting the 'dawning sun' and thus having the same effect as more recognizable sun symbolism. Often in the visual effects designs on the screen, you'll notice animation that simulates a light source radiating momentarily from behind the TV station logo or news show logo. Or you'll frequently just see sunrays emanating from an unseen sun. You'll definitely notice sunrays on the national and local news within their set design.

Pop Illuminati Challenge! Find three examples of a major corporate or brand name logo that does *not* have at least one of the 18 symbols listed above incorporated into its design.

The sun or rising sun symbolizes the dawning of a new day. That is to say, the dawning of a New World Order. The symbolism has ancient esoteric roots and has crept up in the New Age movement. Watch this Youtube video of occult researcher Jordan Maxwell for a fascinating (if a bit dry) presentation of the history of the sun symbol, its occult significance, and how it has been used in abundance recently (in Obama's campaign logo, for instance) as a testament of the impending New World Order.

When I became aware of some of this symbolism, I had the TV on and I just started looking. Suns, stars, earth, pyramids, eyes leaped out of the screen at me. Every commercial, every cartoon, every show. The symbols come in the form of lights, illustrations, special effects, the way objects are placed in the frame (mise en scéne), the set décor and design, or some combination of these—in the foreground, in the background, right in front of your face. The CBS logo is an eyeball, and also an eclipse. The feathers of the NBC peacock are really a rising sun.

Pop Illuminati is the infiltration of the Illuminati into the popular culture of a society. The big Eye runs all the major media news outlets, and all the major film and music studio companies, and the major presses, publishing houses, and universities. Let me rephrase that: the Illuminati owns and controls almost all of the pertinent information you receive and have received over your lifespan. And the information your parents received, and that their parents received, and so on.

To deceive and mislead the public, the Illuminati employs a combination of symbolism, subliminal messaging, predictive programming, thought manipulation, subtle and blatant propaganda, reverse psychology, total fabrication of world events and how the United States ties-in to those events.

If one but opens his or her eyes and keeps them open for a while, the gist of what is occurring in our society and world would become clear. We...you and me...are characters of a made-up narrative. Like in a movie, or a drama, or bad TV script. The Illuminati is the author and director. I call this creation, this script, this play, this movie, this matrix: Pop Illuminati.

The *props* of film Pop Illuminati are...buildings, brief cases, space satellites, missiles, Oldsmobiles, traffic lights, gas stations, teeter-totters, black ties, sex toys, television sets, trees, The Mona Lisa, renal dialysis machines, clouds, chemtrails, locomotives, red carpet, grass, surfboards, drones, rosary and anal beads, computers, dollar bills, high heels, dentists' chairs, information, cantaloupes, the rising sun, history textbooks, rain, the *Ipod*, culture, credit cards, all matter that you can see, hear, touch, smell, and taste. The *sets* include: offices, sidewalks, the shopping mall, living rooms, apartments, dorm rooms, lunch lines, bedrooms, parks, classrooms, the prairie, assembly lines, funeral parlors, delivery rooms, McDonalds, bathrooms, museums, soup kitchens, opera houses, outhouses, front lawns, freeways, laundromats, narrow hallways, clear ponds, supermarkets, the Whitehouse, the gutter, the post office, dark alleys, the courtroom, hair salon, bar, parking lot, the tobacco shop, the zoo, the projects, the strip mall, and strip club, and snuff shop, and Sunday school.

The *setting* is present day earth.

The big political players (e.g., U.S. congress, executive branch, campaign running mates) are essentially paid actors pretending to work in politics and make decisions that influence the future course of our nation and its influence in the world, while in actuality the shadow government of the illuminati has the end of the drama written. When Obama delivers a speech, appears in public, and when the Congress pour into their chamber to vote on a bill, it is all performance. When not scripted, then adlibbed within bounds. When you hear on the news about heated words exchanged between Obama and the Speaker of the House having occurred behind the scenes over some made up issue, it is *fake*. There are no bitter words, no interparty conflict (at this level of government), because all of these politicians are bought and put into office by corporations. The corporations are in cahoots with the banksters--the creators of our currency out of thin air which they then charge interest on. If these world bankers, comprising the International Monetary Fund, the World Bank, and the Federal Reserve, are not the Eye at the pyramid's apex, then they've got to be right up close to there, or its most critical tool.

*The governments, the bankers, the networks, the corporation
heads...They are all in bed together. Under the covers. Naked.
Sucking a little dangalang. Eating a bit of pie. Taking a few toes
in the mouth here; getting it in the ass over there.*

*Sixty-nining. Erecting threeway oral pyramids—six-six-sixing
and brown Eye bowing.*

*Tugging hair/ smacking face/ flicking ballsack!
Nipples, needles, and red milk.*

*...a salad-tossing competition...
Squatting over heads-
...and shitting on faces.*

**By: Wazul L. Lulavellaelli--Social critic, prose-poet,
essayist, humanitarian, Masonic craftsman of fine
silver bullet and durable wooden stake products.
Selection from: *Shitting on Faces and Other
Satirical Prose-Poems* (Great Flock Press, 1971).**

The New World Order onset is palpable in
American society. As the world as we know it nears its
demise, more and more people are awakening to the
matrix. This is largely due to the advancements in and
accessibility of computer technology, including the
advent of social networking websites such as Youtube
and Facebook. This has also led to an explosion of
alternative media programs, such as Alex Jones's radio
show dedicated to investigating the New World Order
conspiracy (www.infowars.com). But it's also because as
conditions in our country and the world worsen the
people are starting to open their eyes to what's
happening around them, and open their minds to

consider alternative perspectives on the way our social world works.

"There's something wrong in the world today, I don't know what it is. Something's wrong with our eyes...."
~ **Aerosmith, "Livin' on the Edge" from the album** *Get a Grip* **(1993)**

The Illuminati, the control freaks that they are, want to control the opposition. Knowing ahead of time that in these perilous times people will start rousing awake (in fact, the conditions program them to do so), the Illuminati wants to control this mass awakening. It appears they've thought it prudent to *slowly* stir our society from its slumber. You can't just one day, if you're the Illuminati, say "alright, you American fuckers...We've been fucking with you all along, now get your raunchy red-white-and-blue lovin' ass in that FEMA camp or we'll release some nerve gas from those 'jet streams' you see crisscrossing in the sky every day." The American people would not know how to act. They'd probably think it was a joke or become immobilized. So the Illuminati wrote the so-called Truther movement into the program. Introducing their agenda insidiously.

They see it necessary for American people to be primed to recognize this NWO coup. This is the purpose for all the hidden symbolism and predictive programming. It informs people's unconscious minds that they've been duped this whole time and people subconsciously submit, in turn preparing the people to consciously acknowledge the reality of the NWO conspiracy.

Operating in the shadows, the Illuminati heads all of the alternative media outlets propagating anti-illuminati sentiments. Hence, we come upon another level of the same Pop Illuminati video game. The Illuminati uses alternative media and Youtube to target those who are already awake or in the awakening process—it misleads them, making them suppose, for instance, that the NWO agenda is engineered by extraterrestrial beings, or that Obama is the Antichrist (I'm not refuting either of these two assertions, by the way). Baffling us by way of constructing hundreds of differing theories also serves to keep the awakened in strife and impedes any real progress on our part. It's a tactic the Illuminati has always utilized: get and keep the masses fighting with each other by accepting and defending positions, while they progress in establishing their New World Order.

More chilling is the degree of interactivity of these social networking discussion boards (e.g., of Youtube or Facebook). You can bet if you participate in debating on the discussion boards, you have a secret profile constructed of you. And a database. Organizing your likes, dislikes. Personal choices, aspirations, limitations, social skills, marriage status, college, job, your photos, your family's photos, your biggest fears (anyone who's read George Orwell's *1984* knows what this information in the wrong hands can get you). The more controversial or correct your views or posts are, the more heat you'll get on you. Facebook NWO conspiracy groups and posters on Youtube videos are often shills….people pretending to be on the side of the awakened but misleading folks. And more shills are creating their own Youtube videos that call-out individual Youtube posters, appearing to threaten them.

Pop Illuminati is a grand virtual video game. We believe we hold the controller, but we are really only the game's protagonist. A character. This holds true always to some degree even after we are aware of the NWO agenda. This small bit of knowledge garners us some degree of control, assuming the adage "knowledge is power" holds any legitimacy. On the other hand, it is conceivable that awareness of the game is in actuality another game level and the increased control you believe you procured via this new awareness is merely a delusion of your game's character. Hell, as far we know, there may not be a 'real you' beyond the game's character. Maybe your life began with the start of the game and ends when the game cartridge is pulled out.

Let's break it down a bit.

You wake up. You know you have to be at work in one hour. Your motivation becomes completing all the required steps that will get you from point A (home) to point B (work) on time. You did not create these steps. They were imposed on you from society. You suddenly take up a role. The role of, say, a postal worker rushing to fulfill his duties of the day. You get to work, you become a postal worker fulfilling his daily duties. You go home, slip into a slightly modified role--a wife, or father. You may play a student. You may be self-employed and fulfill the role in accordance with running a business. You subconsciously choose movies and television programs depicting the life you either think you have or the life you want to have. In given situations, you model the characters based on what they would do in the situation. You may think back to how Ward Cleaver would have handled Beaver, for instance. You might try to discipline your children in a calm, rational consoling tone as well, momentarily fulfilling your Ward Cleaver role. Later you feel the high heeled shoes of a sexual deviant, perhaps, digging into your chest. At bedtime, you take on the role of "a guy turning in." You are sitting there right now playing the role of a skeptic. You may believe that you are being skeptical because you are wise. The reality is that all of your doubts and counterviews are a result of past conditioning. Past learning. Propaganda. Programming. Brainwashing. Mind raping.

Pop Illuminati made you the skeptic you are today.

Every story 'reported' on the news and in the newspapers serves as a catalyst for the New World Order agenda. It serves to scare ("Increase in Flu related deaths in children"), terrorize ("Attempted Bombing of Subway Train Stopped"), incite conflict ("President Obama to Propose New Gun Control Plan"), mislead ("New Report: Economy Not Bad"), confuse ("Thousands of Dead Birds Drop From the Sky"), distract ("Prince William to Marry Hot Piece of Ass"), empower ("National Defense Authorization Act Signed By Obama While Your Drunken Ass Was Bringing in the New Year Acting Foolish, Puking and Pissing On Your Self And Screwing Your Wife's Slutty Syphilitic Sister Over An Arbitrary Date Change") and much more.

The Illuminati continually creates and recreates society and the individual. Your style. Your values. The personality. All subcultures. They created conservatives and liberals. Lower class, middle class, upper class. Hippies, yuppies. Crypts, Bloods. Feminists, Nazis. The Tea Party. Wall Street Occupiers, communists, and gangsta rap. Brittany Spears fans (there had to be an external cause). They made Vanilla Ice haters by virtue of making Vanilla Ice. In short, the Illuminati has created a world of assholes.

The Democratic Party exists to make you feel as though you have a strong alliance in support of the working person's interest. You feel comradeship. When really the party is another manipulation tool. You see legislation passed that appears to favor you, so you have learned to trust the high-ranking Democrats in office. You see them as "one of us." They are far from it. They are "one of them." People should be opening their eyes and seeing through this grand deception as our government's actions become increasingly bogus and outlandish.

Other political parties--e.g., the Tea Party, Libertarians--serve identical, hidden functions.

But it gets deeper, subtler, and sleazier. We are also brainwashed in how much we will tolerate as U.S. citizens. Our tolerance threshold for bullshit, bullying, lying, submission, and the outrageous expands with each passing year. An example: more Americans now seem ready to passively accept U.S. led wars as no big thing (evidence? Who's fighting tooth and nail against U.S. invasions and occupations, so that it would make a discernible difference? Were not both the Democrat and Republican presidential nominees in 2012 for preemptively attacking Iran?). What American would stand for this shit pre-911? Can you think of other bullshit tolerated that wouldn't have been in years past? I'm sure you can.

My awakening experience happened when I'd lost my job a couple years back. During my six months of looking for work, living off my 401K fund and laughable amount of unemployment income, in my spare time (not many job openings in my small town) I perused Youtube. Looking into videos on 911 being an inside job and conspiracy documentaries such as Dylan Avey's original *Loose Change* (2005) opened my eyes. The initial awakening happened in a discernible flash of understanding. The horror, confusion, depression, fear, anxiety, and exhilaration increased with each new piece of information obtained. Watching videos and reading information online became my compulsion. My entertainment. My life. I stopped writing for awhile. I recall times of going days without sleeping, just being online, absorbing this new fascinating knowledge. I felt a bit privileged to understand it, and be in the "know." This evolved into what non-awakened folks might call self-righteousness. And, in a sense, they are correct.

What's perhaps been most challenging in my 'journey to illumination' is sorting out truth from myth....i.e. cutting through the bullshit. For the awakened to be of any pragmatic use to our society we need to—once collecting and evaluating the evidence— learn to think for ourselves. Otherwise, it's all just more brain-garbage. (Is it even possible to think for one's self?) Furthermore, conspiracy theorists need to do their best to locate primary sources, rather than taking at face value what Alex Jones, or David Icke, or the Truther Girls, or a Youtube poster says are in these sources. And we should always consider the source ....but is it even possible to find a 100% reliable news/information source? Should we just take The Associated Press's word over what an independent, awakened investigator uncovers, automatically? Can we trust professional science journals?

They've already tossed us out to spoil-rot. And, the most painfully tragic part may be that we offer our children to that...that big fucking Eye. To serve It. To play an instrumental role in facilitating it's NWO agenda, under the ironic pretense that the young soldier is defending freedom, peace, and liberty--the American democratic way of life. And the stakes have risen. His lovely wife is expecting. He'll be damned if his kid grows up stunted beneath the oppressive regime of an Islamic extremist theocracy. His first tour in Iraq and he has just sacrificed his own eye to the cause of the big Eye in a brief, explosive '*pop*'—the sudden intrusion of a sand nigger's bullet. The soldier's fatigued buddy glimpses over and sees the large clod of blood and guck eject from the soldier's face within the blur of the dawning sun. The hit soldier spins and drops in the sand. The friend who watched it never saw anybody shot before. Raw terror fills him and the auburn sky zaps him of his breath. No opposition for days. It's an ambush. Gun fire erupting like a supervolcano. His friend is screaming, but he can't move to help him. No, he can. He doesn't want his own eye getting blown out of its socket. It's safer here. Behind this...thing. *Coward.* That's another...that's some other hit soldier who's screaming his dying lungs out. On...a battlefield, somewhere. He drops to the floor and rolls around in the glitter. A young kid wrestling with his brother and sister. The fireworks display outside the opened living room window showers the sky with beautiful sparkles.

His mom brings in PB&J sandwiches and cherry Kool-aid. So young and gorgeous. He feels those warm stiff feelings, long repressed.

"Love you, mom."

"Love you, *Wingnut.*"

She knows his army nickname. But she succumbed to her liver cancer while he was in high school. At the window pane, Wingnut watches in awe as luminous giant flowers sprout in bursts in the night sky. A green bud gives birth to a glimmering purple daisy. Within the cacophony of bangs and pops someone cheers continuously and with great vigor at the wondrous pyrotechnics display. Who can blame him? Wingnut recognizes the voice. Shimmering gold and silver sunflower pedals stretch to long jagged cracks of light. Fading. Explosions of sparks spiraling, expanding. They settle to form a huge eye. It's that of an old friend, and now Wingnut places the disembodied voice. His old war buddy lies beneath a pile of dirty laundry in a corner of the living room--shrieking in ecstatic appreciation of the spectacle that Wingnut's mom invited him over to watch.

The hazel eye alone remains gleaming in the sky when a firework ignites at the pupil, discharging a torrential fountain of red sparkles and obliterating the eye. His friend can't get enough of it.

Wingnut still has nightmares of his dead one-eyed soldier pal creeping fiendishly into his bunker to remove an eye from his sleeping head…to, you know, replace the eye demolished by the sand nigger's bullet. Jolting awake, he grips the side of his face, screaming, trembling, sobbing. And shitting the covers.

"An eye for an eye makes the whole world blind."
~**Mohandis "Mahatma" Gandhi**

With the help of the politically correct labels "conspiracy buff" and "conspiracy enthusiast,' the Elite has conditioned the public to perceive those having a more passive interest in conspiracy theory information- -i.e., those who don't buy into the NWO conspiracy--as being "buffs" much the same way that one is a "WW2 buff" or a movie buff. Conspiracy theory has become a "subject" that can be learned by anyone interested.
What's more is the "Illuminati" and "New World Order" subjects are grouped with other fringe interests...the New Age, UFO phenomena, The Bermuda Triangle, ghosts, ancient mysteries, astrology, the apocalypse, the Occult...and often blurred with these other subjects (thank you, David Icke, Alex Jones, Jordan Maxwell, half the truthers on the internet, me). While it is true that the Illuminati may to some extent relate with any of these other subjects or phenomena (this sentence a function of my own conditioning), it need not for it to be a real threat. And so there are Trekkies, gamers, Rocky Horror Picture Show cultists, paranormal researchers, Tarot readers, Bizarro fiction fans, stoners, and conspiracy theorists (or the gentler "buffs"). Plenty of 'geek-and-freak-tainment' to go around.

Spud sits in his easy chair, shifting the blocks of the small pyramid structure--about the size of a Rubik's Cube-- in his hands, attempting to align each of the 13 layers with the correct colors. Within five minutes, Spud solves it. Most people can't. But I've always considered Spud a genius. From the apex the swirly violet vapor is emitted and Spud sucks it through his lips and holds it in his lungs for ten seconds before exhaling. He's deeply relaxed. He passes me the 'pyd.' I suck in the vapor, holding it. I glance at two legs sticking out of from beneath one of Spud's end tables. The pants are lavender and the feet are in penny loafers.

"Who's that?" I say, blowing out swirly green vapor.

"I dunno," Spud says. "Came home, he was like that."

"Some guys get it bad." I pass him the pyramid.

"Yep," hitting from the pyd.

We sit quietly for several seconds.

"You have a tail now?" I say.

"Nah, man. That's Steve."

I see it was his green python all along. It slithers slowly up his neck, and drapes over his shoulders. And goes limp.

"Did he just die?" taking the pyd.

"Nah. He asleep."

"Oh." I hit it, and suck in deep, holding it.

His front door opens and someone walks in. It's familiar, but I just don't want to say anything. But Spud, eyes glazed, doesn't say anything--doesn't even look up as the man identical to me walks in and stops in the middle of Spud's living room. Even dressed like me, only he's wearing a black ball cap instead of a white one.

"What's going on, Spud?" I say.

"Ain't me." He takes a toke, staring off.

Finally I walk out.

"I didn't stay long," I say.

"You made you nervous. Sit." Spud passes me the pyramid.

I fling myself down on the loveseat where I was sitting. I toke.

Spud's eyes inexplicably turn feline for a moment, as they sometimes will. His afro has two rubber bands wrapping the hair, as usual, creating two large rounded poofs upon his head, making him appear like a very tall Mickey Mouse. All who know him suspect he walks on stilts, concealed beneath his slacks. But no one wants to insult him for fear of getting beat by one of them. So we keep our mouths shut. We also try not to laugh when he walks--he toddles with his legs spread apart, never bending his knees and reminding one of the compasses that you used in geometry class.

He keeps his small apartment relatively tidy, with the occasional fuzz ball on the blue carpet here and there. But it usually smells like a dried dirty sponge. There's no TV. A couple easy chairs and a couch face around an old nicked up wooden coffee table, and there are a couple end tables and some lamps with shades that don't match. On the brown panel walls are several hangings: a framed school photo of Spud in the second grade, wearing black framed glasses and his afro is parted to the side; an Indian dream catcher rigged up like a basketball hoop; an old Stroh's *clock that lights up, the fifty cent rummage sale label still stuck to it; a large promo poster of the 1993 film* Searching for Bobby Fisher *scotch taped to the wall, warped from a large brown water stain; and an original Hieronymus Bosch painting which Spud swears on his mother's grave is authentic. On the coffee table are spread some magazines: a* High Times, *a couple* Hustlers, *a* Big Black Butts, *and one called* Reptiles, Sharks, and Cobras.

"Who the fuck is that?" I motion toward the two legs and penny loafers I see jutting out from beneath one of his end tables.

"He was already smoked." holding his vapor.

"But, who is he?"

He lets it out, and just looks at me. If he heard me, I can't tell. He tosses the python across the room and it lands on its belly in its aquarium sitting on a corner table and it starts slithering frenetically around in it, rattling.

"I thought Steve was a python," I say.

"He rattle sometimes," Spud says.

We exchange several hits off the pyd.

"How's the book comin'?" he says.

"Slow," I say. "Man, need some insight. Ever score that Pandora's Box?"

"Nope. Ain't heard from The Barber. Probably be hearin' somethin' in a couple days."

"Straight." I toke.

"I don't trust that mother fucker, though."

"Barbie?"

"Striped bastard. I think he stole my kidney."

I burst out in giddy laughter.

"That shit ain't funny."

I stop laughing. "Oh. Seriously?"

"Man, look." He lifts up the side of his Jimi Hendrix t-shirt, exposing a scar about ten inches high. "How the hell's an appendix gonna need a slice that big?"

I recall running into him in the Hospital elevator, after Spud's surgery. He was carrying a small cooler.

"Are you the Barbie?" I said.

"It's Barber. My name is The Barber." The Barber is a middle aged robust man, but kind of short. Just taller than I. He wears a navy blue porkpie hat, usually a blazer clashing with a buttoned down shirt with a butterfly collar, which hangs over the blazer. His pants are often plaid, typically not matching the rest of his clothes. He might have looked sharp in the 1960s. His face is always painted like an old style barbershop pole--all white with diagonal red and blue stripes.

He looked annoyed. I saw a paperback sticking out from his blazer pocket. "What trash you reading?" I pulled the book out. "The Great Flock of a New World Order by Jack Lutz. Any good?"

"Stop grabbing," he snatched the book back. "I once cut up a man's face for doing that."

"Sorry Barbie."

He shot me an angry look.

"Did your face just spin?" I said, and the elevator doors parted.

"No, my face did not spin. It's paint. How could my head spin? Now if you'll excuse you, I have a dame to maim." He tugged at his suspenders with his thumbs momentarily, picked up the cooler, and exited the elevator in a flash.

"He had a cooler, huh?" says Spud.

"From what I recall. It looked like a cooler."

"Slimy bastard."

There is a long silence.

"Why am I a slimy bastard?" I ask.

"The Barber. The Barber's a slimy bastard."

"Oh. I know. I ran into him when you got your surgery."

"Man, give me that." Spud leans over and snatches the pyd out of my hands.

"Man, what the fuck?"

"Chill out on this shit. You hittin' too hard." He settles in his chair and hits off the pyramid. "I know his face be spinnin' sometime," blowing swirly, green vapor.

A long pause. "Whose?"

Our society is grotesque. It's sick and decadent and insane. Remember we are products of the Illuminati. Pop Illuminati is their brainchild. As above so below?

"Consumption...I get down on my knees."
~ZZ Top, "Consumption" from the album *La Futura* (2012)

Our consumer culture is a reflection of American corporatism. We behave like a bunch of greedy pigs concerned only about ourselves and our own, no different from the indifferent richest one percent. When we buy a Walmart toy for our child, we push to the back of our minds the inhumane treatment of the sweat shop workers overseas who made the toy, although we were disheartened by the story we saw on TV about it last week.

"But it's different. The masses are just trying to survive," you might have just said to yourself. "The rich have all they need *and* want the luxuries too," you may have just continued on. "If I ever won that much money I would stop at the necessities. I would not loot the lower classes." On a roll. "The rich created this. I behave like this because of *them.*"

You are catching on to Pop Illuminati.

Pop Illuminati Challenge! Was the 'Pick Three' of the Illinois Lotto really the numbers '666' on November 5th 2008, the day after Barack Obama--then Illinois Senator--was elected for his first four year term as our President of the United States?

Two cockroaches fuck on the coffee table. I pretend not to notice so as to not embarrass Spud.

"You havin' those death fears?" he says.

"Yep."

"Afraid you gonna die before you finish writing the book." He hits off the pyd.

I'm slow to respond. "Must be a common fear."

"I doubt it."

I let out a long sigh.

"Cheer up, man. Got somethin' for ya."

Spud pulls out from under his easy chair a small ornate chest, roughly the size of a cigar box.

"Is that...?"

He smiles, then laughs. "What I tell you, man. Told you I got the connection."

"Pandora!"

He sets it on the end table next to him and I skip over the coffee table, open it, and stick my face in. Through lumpy, garish mush, I'm staring over a football field with a lot of ungodly activity taking place. I'm tugged back.

"Man, what the fuck's wrong with you?" Spud is clasping my shoulders. "You can't just be sticking your face in the shit. You wanna die?"

"How are you supposed to take it?" I feel dizzy and violated.

"Foo, you s'pose to open it just a crack and suck in and close it real quick. Man, you okay? You--"

Spud keeps talking. I think. I see The Barber before me, surrounded by a swarm of flies.

"Do you think I'd make a better super hero or a villain?" says The Barber.

"You're not even kidding, are you," I say.

"Hey, with a name like The Barber?" sticking his palms out.

Our whole value-system, our whole idea of what can and should be achieved by human endeavor and what constitutes 'the real world' is controlled by them. It's called social framing, and can be manipulated.

There is a misconception, via social programming, that grand conspiracies only occur in fiction. We have been brainwashed further to believe that people in power in our government could never be so *evil* as to systematically deceive, plot against, manipulate, and murder their own people. Shit. You are not their 'people.' You are peasants. Serfs. Recall sitting through history class hearing stories about kings in medieval times torturing and killing their own people? Why would you think that just because times have changed and we are advanced in technological and scientific know-how that human nature has changed? Did you honestly believe those holding power (e.g., the framers of the U. S. constitution) were just going to one day give up all their power to the masses?

Our ignorance is probably the most powerful weapon used against us.

"Sharp jacket," says Spud.

"Thanks." I extend my arms a bit, checking out the sleeves of the brown leather blazer, a little long." Got it from Goodwill. Still had the tags. Was called a hippy jacket in the 70s, I guess."

"Start callin' you Barbie," he hits off of Pandora's box.

"Fuck that, man. I was retro before that douche.. It was only eight bucks."

"Chill. I'm jivin'. It getchoo any pissy?"

"Not trying, right now."

"Getchoo some pissy."

"I might try and get some pissy."

"Why you so skinny?" He passes me the box in exchange for the pyd.

"Diet." I crack it open and suck in the lumpy mushy garish swirly vapor.

"What kind?"

"Ascetism."

"What, choo mean anorexia nervosa?"

I don't respond.

"Let me get you a granola bar." He starts to stand.

"You get me a granola bar it will be the last thing you do, darky!"

Spud looks surprised. Then wounded. He plops down. 'Compass' legs sprayed.

"Sorry," I say.

"Shit. I know where it comes from. Fuck it. Still, you lucky you my boy or I'd take it out on yo' ass."

The room is blood spattered. Then not.

"You like snickerdoodle?" says Spud.

Pop Illuminati Challenge! What language do the three vertical markings of the *Monster* energy drink represent? How do the three marks translate to English?

Hollywood

"I enjoy playing the audience like a piano."
~Alfred Hitchcock

The Elite likes doing the same with us. As Morpheus in *The Matrix* (1999) said, "People are so dependent on the system that they'll fight to preserve it." You point out the Sandy Hook reference in *Dark Knight Rises* (2012), among several other coincidences that would make Sir Arthur Canon Doyle shit his grave, to anyone who is just willing to look at it and digest it….and they'll soon dismiss it and go on with their lives. The Heads love this, of course. People want to be accepted. Very few want to rock the boat. And people can even start doubting and reverse their perception of what is plainly right before their eyes when the social pressure is intense enough.

Any Hollywood movie that you see is NWO propaganda in one guise or another. Some much more obvious. Perhaps this variability in conspicuousness aims at multiple levels of the unconsciousness or different populations of people. Let's look now at some popular instances of obvious illuminati propaganda and/or symbolism in Hollywood movies.

"Bush knocked down the towers...Tell the truth, nigga!"
~Lyrics to "Bin Laden" by Immortal Technique (2005)

Michael Moore's documentary *Fahrenheit 911* (2004) first implanted the seed that there might be a conspiracy implicating our federal government in the events of the September 11th, 2001, "terrorist attacks." It really did seem implausible that the 'Bushes" alone could have carried it out, however. I now realize that Moore's movie was propaganda (i.e.: "Look at Moore and these other 'conspiracy theorists.' They are nuts and lie. As if the incompetent George W. Bush, who can't even hold a dog in his arms without dropping it, let alone run our government, could carry out 911.") Yet, Bush Jr. might as well have done it. It was on his watch, wasn't it?

Two former U.S. Presidents, their Vice Presidents, and a former U.S. Secretary of Defense all sit about a raging bonfire, roasting marshmallows over the heap of some 14,000 charring copies of Ray Bradbury's fictional masterpiece Fahrenheit 451. Seard, various colored bird feathers sporadically blow about. The five men sit on the sand in lawn chairs in the midst of scattered scraps of burnt rotted dead bird structures, remnants of a humongous glorious vibrant pyramid. Looming in the distance is a monolithic monument of four historic Presidents with sprouting demonic bird faces, Mount Rushmore being its earthly counterpart.

"Ironic, huh?" says Bill Clinton to the other four folks. "What we're doing here. Burning the definitive American classic on tyrannical book burning, in a tyrannical manner. Whataya say, Rummy? Ironic?"

"Yeah, ironic, Bill," Donald Rumsfield finally answers, dryly.

"God damn it is," muses Clinton, pulling his crispy marshmallow from the fire, blowing on it. "Ironic as hell."

'Stupid fucks,' Gore thinks to himself, letting his marshmallow melt to ashy goo drooping from the end of his stick. Even Bill, the only one he remotely cares for among them. The other men present he detests for various reasons, not least being he and his family having to share a shabby two-story four bedroom farmhouse with six other men and their families. He's constantly tormented by ruminations of how he ended up in his present hellish predicament. He was former Vice President to then President Bill Clinton and despite his tumultuous effort to succeed his boss's post, he was barely beat (not by popular vote) by George "911" Bush Jr.. There'd been controversy in the ballot count.....'hanging chads' and so forth. Gore now understands the conspiracy behind that election with its associated drama and twists. He was ordered by superiors to refrain, foolishly, from conceding right away. It was all insidiously designed by the

Illuminati, of course. Even his own motives and aspirations. He thought his ambition was his own. Instead his tireless work ethic and passionate advocacy for environmental issues had been programmed into his brain. Alas, his free-will has been a delusion and probably continues to be controlled--an epiphany that anguishes him daily. He had no Illumination. No privileged insight. He was another worker, instrument, a tool, a disposable resource...a flesh and bone robot....programmed and activated for the express purpose of advancing the Illuminati's not-so-secret-anymore New World Order agenda. And now his utility is obsolete.

He gazes up at the maroon sky. The stars all file into pentagram formation directly above the five of them, and then disperse to their designated stations within the sky. He looks about. No one else was paying attention. Or he hallucinated it. Bush Jr., sporting his white cowboy hat, hangs half out of his chair--drunk as Otis and humming a Hank Williams Sr. tune. Loony lush.

Gore, swigging his brandy, screws on the lid and gazes off into the large, swirling bonfire, wondering who or what the fuck he is.

Bush Sr. is wheeled up to the fire by Colin Powell. He doesn't look quite as pale, now, at night, and his eyes are looking alert and sharp as they had before his kidney transplant. Yet, bags remain beneath them, peppered with small puss filled lumps, some of them oozing. He sees Bill scrutinizing him, and Bill quickly looks away. Bill knows Papa Bush sensed him checking out his appearance. Bush Sr. is as smart as they come. Papa Bush reaches his arm from under a quilt, taking from Powell a stick piercing a marshmallow, and then orders him to go indoors and give Barbara a good balling.

"Yes sir. Will do, sir. The pleasure is mine, sir. Good evening, sir." Powell shuffles in the direction of the farmhouse set

in the valley beyond the patch of woods. He'd likely be shot in the back of the head if Bush Sr. heard the contents of his grumbling.

'Exceedingly better he than I,' Bush Sr. thinks. He used to not mind sex with Barbara, used to even kinda love her at one time. But over the past...twenty years, he hasn't been able to stomach the thought of that welted, withering, fungled, chilly vagina, and of sliding his horse cock into it. 'Like humping cottage cheese.' Then, invariably, the room---hell, the whole goddamn house--inexplicably would reek of boiling cauliflower for two days. The aroma would not be present during the sex act. It started about an hour after they'd done been dressed and were in the middle of a game of chess. Everyone in the farmhouse knew what had happened, by that smell. It was humiliating. Bush Sr. would detect jokes here and there, behind his back. He overheard a scathing one from Bernanke four months ago. That's why he killed him. He instantly shifted into his demonic bald eagle shape and tore him to shreds with his humongous talons in under a minute. He sauntered to the fridge, still in eagle form, removed a bottle of Cackalacky Sauce *with the talon beneath his enormous wing, and poured a generous portion of the spicy sauce onto Bernanke's raw liver and ravenously ate it. This occurred in front of all the men, standing in the kitchen. Their silent expressions of absolute horror and utter terror lasted through-out Papa Bush's brief brunch. His rage had been grossly exaggerated--a brutal action performed mostly for effect: Papa Bush has overheard no more cauliflower jokes. Well, he has, but now they're at Powell's expense, who incidentally has four inches on Bush Sr. During those occasions, the cauliflower smell is all but deadly. Papa Bush has learned to stomach the smell but the sex causing it had to stop. Barbara has never once mentioned the cauliflower smell (assuming she can sense it) and believes Papa Bush is not wise to the infidelity.*

To all the men present at tonight's book burning, he says sternly but calmly:

"I feel as good as I've ever felt. Better, in fact. The Great Flock has ensured that. So everyone back the fuck off."

"Hey, Papa Bush. When's the next book burning?" asks Clinton.

"Do we have all The Great Flock of a New World Order copies, yet?"

"Almost, Papa," says Cheney. "The Vatican has one. And two others are unaccounted for."

"Well, find them. The Vatican can keep their copy."

'Vatican can keep their copy...' thinks Gore. 'As if he'd have the muscle to shakedown even the Pope.'

"Believe me, Papa, we're trying," says Cheney.

"Not hard enough," says Bush Sr. "Better get The Barber on this one. His record for obtaining things is impeccable."

"Do we really need The Barber, Papa?" says Rummy. "With all due respect, I think he's--"

"Forget it, Rummy. It's The Barber or your dick," his eyes turning severe.

Rummy sighs. "I'll summon him." He shudders. When The Barber brought Papa's new kidney, he's convinced he saw that man's head rotate. He hasn't told a soul.

"Minus the castration option, I-I think I have to agree with Rummy on this one, Papa," says Cheney. "The Barber's a stand-up guy, no doubt, but I hear his head swirls."

"It doesn't swirl," mutters Bush Jr.

"Old wives tail," chimes Clinton.

"That's right...old wives tail," agrees George Bush Sr. "And while we're at it, let's kill the author." He glances at the cover. "Bring me the head of Jack Lutz."

"Why do you want his head?" asks Gore.

"Goddamn it, Al!" snaps Bush Sr. (Cheney--seated next to him--flinches.) "You read the book. Don't tell me, goddamn, you weren't humiliated! The man ruined us."

All men present--with the exception of Bush Jr. who's

inebriated and mumbling to himself--gaze at their surroundings in silence for several seconds.

"Uh, we would, Papa, but..." Cheney looks uneasily at Rummy.

Rummy clears his throat. "What Dick is incompetently attempting to tell you, Papa, is that we're not even sure the man exists. 'Jack Lutz' is likely a pen name."

"A pen name..." Bush Sr. stares at him. "What's his real name?"

"Our intelligence is looking into it."

"Do you have anything on him?"

"Sorry, Papa." Rummy looks at the ground.

Bush Sr.--flustered--says: "Well...bring me the rest of his books. Who's the publisher?" flipping to the front pages, grumbling 'goddamns'. He finds it, looks up at Rummy, then at Bill, then Cheney. Bush Jr. is passed out in the lawn chair. He looks at Al Gore, who doesn't even show the respect to look back at him. He looks back down at the words: Great Flock Press. *He looks again up at Rummy. "This a joke?"*

"Afraid not, Papa," says Rummy.

"The publishing house is named after the Order? Our Order?"

"I was thinkin'," starts Bill Clinton, "perhaps someone inside our Great Flock-- well, our once great flock---was ordered to put this book out."

"Ordered by who?"

"I wasn't talkin' to you, Rummy. I was talkin' to Papa Bush."

"Sor-ree," Rummy retorts.

"Well, butt-out," says Clinton, and from nowhere a fist jabs him square in the jaw, jarring him.

The fist belongs to Papa Bush, who has risen from his wheelchair on his scrawny, wobbly legs. His arm remains extended, and his quilt is wadded around his ankles in the sand, exposing his plaid boxers. He says, "Watch your fucking mouth on the Order, boy. Hone your respect. This is the Order of Nevermore, remember that?!"

Clinton's face is beet red. "Y-yes, Papa B-bush." Bush Sr. stares him down, and finally Bill mopes to his lawn chair and sits. Rummy's cheeks bulge with suppressed laughter as he bites his lip so hard that he tastes blood. Gore is fuming on the inside. Dick looks frightened.

As quickly as Bush Sr. lost his composure, he regains it, and resumes sitting calmly in his wheelchair. Rummy helps him with the quilt.

Gore stands up and starts shouting: "This is bullshit! A man writes a book and we're forever trapped in this wasteland! We find that Lucifer is but another pawn. Zacherly gets cast out. I was supposed to be a master of my own world. Now I'm stuck listening to you assholes all night, every night. Roasting fucking marshmallows. You're all delusional! Clinging to some twisted fantasy of reality. A reality that I don't even know how to begin comprehending!"

Bush Sr. looks about passively. "Hear something, Rummy?"

"Negativity," he answers.

Papa Bush nods. "Take care of it?"

"No. Wait, now," says Gore.

"Gladly," Rummy pulls the 13 mm from the front of his khaki shorts and blasts Gore's brains all over the fire.

A chunk of skull lands in Bush Jr.'s beer. "Damn Gore..." he grumbles, picking it out. Taking a drink.

Bill's blood speckled face expresses terror. Cheney starts crying.

To Rummy, Bush Sr. says, "These alternative authors...some are getting too close to the truth. Someone is going to nail it."

Startled, Rumsfeld stares frantically about. "You hear that?"

"What?"

"I don't know....Ever get the feeling we're being watched?"

Bush Senior looks inquisitively up at the maroon sky. Then at the harvest moon. "You drink too goddamn much." He knocks the glass of brandy out of Rummy's hand.

There were 911 premonitions in the movies. Near the end of *Fight Club* (1999) the protagonist and his wife hold hands, their bodies forming an "M" (for Mason) as they stare out a high rise window and watch the skyscrapers of the fictional city disintegrate and collapse, the last two being twin towers. Notice, further, the spot of light in the background moving in the direction of the towers. Could this be symbolic of an airplane? In *Hackers* (1995) two characters look to the World Trade Center Twin Towers seated by a window in a restaurant. Both towers are lighted up in words: one stating "Crash" the other "Burn."

Cartoons got in on the premonition fun. In a *Simpsons* episode from 1997, Bart holds a wad of cash in front of a cartoon magazine cover that depicts a large number '9' positioned on the left side of the twin towers (these symbolizing the number '11'). The wad of cash represents the blood money collectively made by the world's wealthiest in the wake of the attacks.

As far back as 1983, we see a 911 reference in the smash hit comedy *Trading Places* (Directed by John Landis), starring Eddie Murphy and Dan Ackroyd. The story is interestingly about a couple rich fat cats using their resources and cunning to turn the incredibly wealthy and snobby Dan Ackroyd character into a poor, homeless guy, in effect trading places with the Eddie Murphy character who becomes the rich successful one. They accomplish this feat overnight, a testament of their great power. The reference comes when the two characters step out of a vehicle and gaze up at the Twin Towers. A subsequent scene inside the World Trade Center shows a clock on the wall—the time is 8:55. In your mind's eye, you should see the face of a clock: one hand pointing to the '9' and the other to the '11.'

In *Terminator 2: Judgment Day* (1991), Arnold Schwarzenegger is on a motorcycle being chased by the bad guy terminator, who's behind the wheel of a big semi rig. Arnold fires his gun behind him, blowing out the bad terminator's tire and sending him crashing head first into the side of a bridge with a sign reading, "Caution 9' 11" (i.e., 9 feet 11 inches). He hits it right at the divider of the two underpasses of the bridge. The shapes of the double tunnels bring to mind twin towers. The fuel leaking from the gas tank of the wrecked rig, subsequently causing it and the bridge to blow up, is a great example of predictive programming. Millions of viewers see this and subconsciously are more accepting of the official cause of the twin towers collapsing— leaked jet fuel igniting.

Most 911 conspiracy theorists believe the Twin Towers were brought down by demolition bombs, or something akin. There's good evidence of this. In case you didn't know or recall, Building 7 was the third world trade center tower that collapsed on 911. But there were only two planes that crashed in Manhattan that day, you say? True. So why did this other building collapse into its own footprint at freefall speed, just as the Twin Towers had?

"Stop this stupid sideshow!"
~**Dr. Seaton in** *Poltergiest III* **(Directed by Gary Sherman, 1988)**

Hollywood's Rule of Triple 6s

"I shot him 6 times, I shot him 6 times.....I shot him 6 times."
~Donald Pleasence as Dr. Loomis, *Halloween II* (Directed by Rick Rosenthal, 1981)

I've heard that all Hollywood movies have the mark of the beast in them. They are supposedly subtle but apparent when paying close attention. I don't know if it is true, as I have not seen all Hollywood movies.

The other night I had a guest over and we watched a few older random DVDs. Three of them: *National Lampoon's Animal House* (Dir. John Landis, 1978) *Austin Powers II: The Spy Who Shagged Me* (Dir. Jay Roach, 1999) and the hilariously horrible *Poltergeist III* (1988). I decided to be mindful of potential 666s.

We watched *Animal House* first. Keeping an eye out for the triple 6s, I caught it. It happens in the scene in which the character Otter takes flowers to the girl who set him up, as several guys from his rival fraternity, Omega Theta Pi, await him at her apartment to kick his ass. At the door, we see apartment number six. The camera cuts twice revealing the same number six on the door. That's 6-6-6.

"That's the fact, Jack."
~Bill Murray in *Stripes* (Directed by Ivan Reitman, 1981)

Next, we popped in *Austin Powers II: The Spy Who Shagged Me*. In Dr. Evil's command center (the set design a bunch of inverted pyramids, incidentally, aiming downward where the lava flows within the volcanic mountain) he says he'll bomb the Earth in six hours. Approximately a second afterwards, Mini-me, Dr. Evil's clone, emphasizes the '*six*' by holding up six fingers twice in a row.

Finally we watched *Poltergeist III*. A scene in a parking garage shows the number *six* painted on the wall in the background. The same *six* is shown exactly two additional times within the scene.

How in the fuck is this coincidence?

Since then, I've discovered the 666 in *My Blue Heaven* (Dir. Herbert Ross, 1990) *Halloween III: Season of the Witch* (Dir. Tommy Lee Wallace, 1982), *Creepshow* (Dir. George Romero, 1982) and many other films. In *Creepshow,* it comes in the form of six candles on the Father's Day cake, "the cake" being a disembodied head with frosting on the top. Three times the camera cuts, revealing the six candles

In a more recent movie, *Chronicle*, the 666 is less obvious. It's near the beginning in the form of a paper folded circular symbol hanging on a door. Six triangles connecting at the corners in a circle. Do you comprehend it? Triangles are three sided, of course. Three times six?

"Heard The Barber cut up some woman the other day," says Spud.

"Really?!"

"Yep," *hitting from Pandora's Box. He passes it.*

I reflect on this. "He cut up her boobies?" *I pass the pyd.*

"Yep. Two-bit hustler thug. Thinkin' he hard. Can't take on a man."

I gently open the Box a crack, and inhale.

A bloody black leather glove lays wadded up on the coffee table. I look at the High Times *magazine next to it. A large pyd is on the cover. On the cover of the magazine next to it the buck naked black girl with the big booty looks at me and says,* "Getchoo some pissy."

"Well, I gotta go," *I tell Spud.* "Lotta shit I got--"

He slams his fist down on the coffee table. "You just don't wanna get beat on checkers."

What am I going to do? I don't want hurt his feelings. Spud is a brilliant checkers player. Though I believe he'd rather be brilliant at chess. He's lousy at the game, which is odd as he's so smart with solving the pyd. One would think both activities would involve the same area of the brain, the part that entails spatial-intelligence. "Break out the board. Got time for one."

He relaxes. Sits back. A half hour goes by. Finally, "Let's roll a 'rillo." *He reaches for the Dutch Master's cigar box and opens Pandora's box instead. He sticks his hand in, and a look of utter horror shows on his face, as he yanks his hand out too fast, knocking the box onto the floor. An odd vapory mush, with mechanical thrashing, buzzing, and thousands of shrieks, falls out of it. He rises, bends down and picks up the mush, not bending his legs. Screaming, he throws it back into the box and slams it shut. His hands are smoldering and covered with spots that look a bit like fresh cigarette burns. Liquid skin runs down his wrists. We never got around to checkers.*

Television

"You see? You see? Your stupid minds. Stupid!
Stupid!"
**~Human looking alien fellow to earthling in
Edward D. Wood Jr.'s** *Plan 9 From Outer Space*
(1956)

You've probably in your life heard someone say
sometime: "I'm gonna turn on the idiot box." And it
was probably a man who said it. Somewhere in his late
50s or so (I have no idea the reason for the correlation).
The person who said this appears to understand that
the television set is an 'idiot box,' yet is fully willing to
turn it on, sit down in front of it for a couple hours,
and let it work its idiotic magic on his brain. You've
also heard the TV called "the boobtube," for the same
reason (no it has nothing to do with boobies). 'Boob' is
a synonym for 'dumb,' of course.

"...better roll with me, *Jack*."
**~ZZ Top, "It's Too Easy Manana" from the
album** *La Futura* **(2012)**

Yes the TV makes us dumber. It manipulates us
into thinking and relating to other people in shallow,
prescribed ways. Probably to a greater extent than any
other Illuminati mass brainwashing tool it constructs
our social frame. Most Americans generally have the
same overall social frame. We are taught to believe
certain things about the world we live in. The earth is
round, America is the greatest nation ever to exist, I
can't walk through this door without opening it first,
work full time, overweight people are buffoons, raise a

family, you are 'somebody,' start a career, go to college, build for retirement, farting in public is embarrassing, trust in the American way of life, Osama Bin Laden is dead, if you work hard it will always pay off, people can't communicate with the dead, we should be at war, we should not be at war, abortion is a woman's choice, abortion is murder, etc., etc., etc....It makes no difference that not all of these things are factual. Some are factual. Mixing truth with deception makes it harder to detect deception (especially when the truth is much more complicated than the narrow views we are taught to take on). The point is that the way we are taught to view and relate to our world is deliberately designed. It's taught to us through our TV and by our parents who learned it from TV and their parents, who learned it from watching TV and from their parents, who learned it from newspapers and radio and their parents.

"[The demon] will mix lies with the truth to attack us. The attack is psychological...and powerful."
~ **Max Von Sydow as Father Merrin in** *The Exorcist* **(1973)**

"What's takin' you so long with the book, man?" Spud passes me the pyd.

"Research." I pass him Pandora's box with shaky hands.

"You don't need to be mixing pyd and Pandora with books."

"It's nonfiction! What the hell else am I supposed to do?"

"Truth is stranger than non-fiction." Spud hits off of Pandora's box held in his bandaged hands. "Heard you got fired again."

"How the hell did you know? It just happened."

"Heard it from The Barber."

"The Barber? I haven't seen Barbie since your surgery. What the fuck, is he omniscient?"

"Must be."

"I'm making half of it fiction."

"How's that?"

"I'm adding real bits from my life, in a fictional guise. The struggle in creating this book."

"That's pretty hip. Shit. Don't put me in it."

"Wasn't planning on it." I hit off the pyramid.

"If that be the case, though, don't misguide anyone. Try to be honest about yourself."

"I don't like exposing myself. I can't come off as self-absorbed."

"How the fuck else you expect people to take you seriously, hick?"

Several cockroaches march out on Spud's carpeting and form a pentagram shape in the center of the room. Spud pretends not to see.

"Been lookin' for another job?" he says.

"It's not easy in this town, you know."

"Don't choo be havin' college degrees?"

"I burned them."

"You crazy."

"Anyway, all jobs, one way or another, ultimately help bring about the New World Order."

"Say what?"

"When you're a kid they ask 'what do you want to be when you grow up?' You hear shit like, 'You can be whatever you want.' But all careers are invented for that sole purpose."

"Foo...you gotta play within the system to beat the system."

"You're telling me to sell-out."

"I'm telling you about beating them at their own game."

"There's a way to beat Pop Illuminati?"

He's either in deep contemplation or has zoned out.

Every show is a program designed for specific tasks. Following are a few examples of TV shows I've come across and what I believe to be the show's central programming message.

King of Queens

TV teaches us a lot about living, being civilized and being a good slave. Look at the zany couple in *King of Queens*. The dude has some shitty nine-to-five delivery truck job that he seems to be content with, and they don't live in luxury and often fight, but they sure fucking enjoy their time off together and have a lot of mundane fun.

The Program: Hey, this is awesome, man! This is how to live. Beer, BBQ, football, goofin'. *Everybody* is supposed to perform mundane, lifeless, soulless, menial, mechanical, dehumanizing work most of the time they are awake, yet still struggle and barely have any time for worthwhile pursuits. Wait, this way of life *is* a worthwhile pursuit. It's the American way! WOOOO!

Seinfeld

Four adult New York friends get together each week for antics and commentary on society's quirks.

The Program: Be aloof to events in your world. Use humor as a defense mechanism for anything that seems 'off' in life and move on with your conventional life. Life and human interaction is all just one big joking laugh riot.

Frasier

I love *Frasier*. It's one of my favorite sitcoms ever. Still, it's a program. It concerns a middle-aged psychiatrist with a Seattle radio call-in show. He's cultured, caring, and seems to be genuinely happy and enjoy life.

The Program: Being a know-it-all pompous snob is a worthy goal in life. Life fulfillment will come if you just...spend your free time learning everything there is to know about art, regularly attend the opera, read and read and read, get smart and learn a bunch of big words, become a wine connoisseur, listen to Bach and read Shakespeare. Also go to college for twelve years and pursue a professional degree. Build your ego.

TV is also used by the Elite to confuse us and induce conflict within ourselves and between one another. There's no shortage of programs displaying steamy scenes of extramarital liaisons and spouses lying and getting away with it. Is there a correlation with the high divorce rate?

If a TV personality has a large enough following, it can be very dangerous. We've seen what a charismatic cult leader can convince his and her disciples to do. Remember the mass suicide in the Heaven's Gate case? How can we be certain the affect that Oprah Winfrey, of the Oprah Winfrey Network (OWN....wink), is beneficial and not detrimental? Is Dr. Phil teaching conformity to the current social structure to his legions of loyal disciples?

Perhaps the affects of the two people mentioned above are too insidious to detect. It's easier to see the propaganda when it's direct, aggressive, and ugly. Take

Bill O'Reilly for instance. This man is a propaganda spewing machine. He's a mouthpiece of Fox News and conservative politics. More people are becoming assholes from watching Bill O'Reilly than from watching anyone else. It's due to people believing and following personalities such as him, Glen Beck, Sean Hannity and Rush Limbaugh that we are at war right now. Americans believed these salesmen enough to go to war and to believe in our current 'cause' of war. We bought what we were sold. And we still are buying it.

Not only do they create the contentious groups they also set the parameters of debates. They create and manipulate the stances you take on controversial topics. Most people are either a creationist or evolutionist (our origin was either God or natural selection), a conservative or a liberal or a moderate. They also make us pick sides on issues that are not black and white. Issues that have arguably equally valid points, and will never be settled, such as abortion. Often they use celebrities that are intelligent, articulate, seemingly informed, and even "anti-establishment' to reinforce the *'nothing-out-of-the-ordinary-happening-here'* mentality. When Marilyn Manson was a guest on The O'Reilly Factor he summed up his interview with an appreciation of living in a free country where we are able to voice and disagree on controversial issues. His fans see this and most just automatically believe—'If Marylin said it, it must be true.'

"More Pandora!" I yell.

"You a mess, man," says Spud. "You ever comb your hair?"

"Pandora!"

"You don't need no more right now. It makin' you crazy."

I clench Spud's T-shirt at his chest, trying to shake him. "Give up the shit, jig!"

"Stop it!" He smacks me. "Get control!" He back hands me. Front hands me. Back hands me.

I drop to his floor. Nose leaking blood, I crawl and pick up my glasses and put them on. Then I climb up onto his couch and sit.

"I ought to drag you out there and FEED you to those things!"
**~ Ben to Cooper in *Night of the Living Dead*
(Directed by George A. Romero, 1968)**

Spud sighs and throws me a hanky. I wipe the blood off my face and hold it to my nose, sitting quietly for about five minutes.

"I don't know what's happening to me."

"You just tweakin'. Let me getchoo a cup a beer."

Spud returns from the kitchen and hands me a chipped teacup. I hungrily drink the warm beer it contains. "Things are coming at me too fast. I can't keep up with 'em."

"One word at a time, Jack."

It's as bad as people not even knowing where their opinions come from. They walk around parroting some fake drama Bill O'Reilly stirs up: "Yeah, Obama should be impeached. He should be impeached. He should be impeached."

When these people fight and defend their political party it is all show--democrat or republican does not make a difference. The two-party system is there for you to pick a side and defend. It's your football team against theirs. But the big players in politics are not on either team. They are playing both sides against one another. If we don't see this then we will continue to blame the damn "republicans" or those damn "democrats" for everything, but not the ones creating the chaos and conflict in our society and the world by creating groups with conflicting interests. And then they instigate shit. They create order out of the chaos they caused.

Divide and conquer.

"Y'Know, Nietzche says, 'Out of chaos *comes* order.'"
"Oh, blow it out your ass, Howard."
~Exchange between Howard Johnson and Olson Johnson in *Blazing Saddles* (Directed by Mel Brooks, 1974)

American sports is another stroke of brilliance by the Illuminati. The rich make money, exploit young players who become stars, and it gives many men reasons for living. It's more distraction, and serves to reinforce the competitive spirit.

I'm not insinuating that the competitive spirit is a bad thing, intrinsically. It is, however, exploited by the Illuminati and a necessary condition for the America deception to operate. The Rich figured out that we would be more efficient slaves in a competitive, capitalist society. Capitalism is an economic system devised by the Elite to get more productivity out of us. They reasoned that if the slaves are given a certain amount of freedom in selecting their occupations, then they should be more productive. But America is a mixed economic system and moving toward communism. This is typical of the Illuminati; over time they mold and remold the societal structure, utilizing what works for the time.

Spud's two afro poofs have morphed into real mouse ears. His python, Steve, has embedded most of its body into the side of Spud's head, leaving about a foot of the snake dangling from the side, whipping about. A snake fang juts out from the temple of the opposite side of Spud's head. His forehead is scaly, the same hue as the python. His eye is greenish red and reptilian.

"Forces are working against me," I say.

"Of course they do," says he.

"My computer, my microwave, my DVD player, my C-PAP machine all gave out within a week of one another. Right now, as we speak, I'm at the library, writing down exactly what you and I say. People are gawking at me suspiciously, I suppose due to my black ball cap. And I carry my shit in a black backpack. Same one I used in college. People are losing their minds with this fake domestic terrorism bullcrap."

"Stand above it, and stop being a pissy. It all be in line with the Cosmic Yin Yang Holomind."

"The what?"

"Was hoping you might know."

"Is it in books?

"Man, you learnt nothing?"

I look at him, befuddled.

"Books, information, symbols--they only guides to truth," he says. "Imperfect representations of reality. Written by man. Foo, truth written before any man try to write it." He opens Pandora's Box a crack and sticks a straw inside. He snort the lumpy vapor up his nostril. "Here." He gestures the box to me, his snake eye gleaming.

"I thought you said--"

"Take it, motha-fucka."

I take the box, crack it open, insert the straw and snort long and hard.. "I'm considering dividing it into two volumes."

This whole conversation took place without either of us opening our mouths.

"You gotta do something." His nose turns snout-like and long whiskers grow out of the sides. He hisses and squeaks, wiggling his forked tongue at me.

He hits from the pyd.

In a particularly disturbing History Channel commercial, small capped pyramid structures are being assembled in a factory and then fly off down the street like airplanes. They pass Mount Rushmore, the Great Pyramid, and other known sites, all the while a poor rendition of the Buddy Holly song "Everyday" ("It's a-gettin' closer") plays. At the commercial's end, one of these 'pyramid planes' hits the side of the 'H' of the History Channel logo. The vertical lines of the "H" represent the two towers. The line adjoining them brings to mind 'conjoined twins.' The History Channel slogan, "Made Every Day" appropriately displays at the commercial's close. The 'hidden' message is clear: We, the Illuminati, make up shit and pass it off as real shit that happened.

Kids read history textbooks today and are told the official 911 story as though it is a fact that has had no controversy. As surely as the earth is round Muslim extremists pulled off this caper with box cutters--and it was masterminded by a bearded dude in a cave in the Middle East. And I have trouble getting my email to work.

I see the creation of new fake history in the making everyday. The newspapers start the shit by nonchalantly and matter-of-factly making reference to interpretations of events as though the interpretations are themselves the events. Let me give you an example. When Obama kept poking his eye to stop 'sincere' tears from flooding his face while first addressing America in the wake of the 'Sandy Hook elementary school shooting,' newspapers would make reference to this event as such: "A very emotional President Obama addressed a mournful nation yesterday...." Do you see a problem? Stating that Obama was emotional conditions the public to believe that Obama was indeed emotional, when in fact he may have been feigning his grief. Both are mere interpretations of the same event. The journalists know what they are doing when they state biased interpretations as fact. A more objective way of making reference to the event would be: "President Obama appeared mournful today...." or "President Obama appeared to be fighting back tears..." It would *seem* the word "appeared" is something of an alchemic neutralizer. If newspapers--a public information dissemination tool--are not reporting events objectively right after they happened, imagine how much more so American history textbooks are not objectively reporting events many, many years after they supposedly occurred.

When a popular conspiracy theorist appears on mainstream television, it's invariably in a negative light. They are usually ridiculed. Often they appear suspiciously to bring it on themselves, as when Alex Jones is guest on The View and goes on a wild rant and makes an ass of himself. When average people bring something up on TV they are often the recipient of intimidation. Bill O'Reilly verbally accosted a 911 questioner who had lost his father in the 'terrorist attacks.' He seems to have a passion for yelling over people and telling them to shut up, further reinforcing the belief that these conspiracy nuts are dangerous and need to be dealt with swiftly, aggressively, mercilessly.

A show like Jesse Ventura's Conspiracy Theory is interesting because it provides a lot of seemingly useful information, but, like all else in Pop Illuminati, viewer beware. The show while fostering greater NWO conspiracy awareness is in all likelihood misleading you. The interactions between Mr. Ventura and his investigative team on the show I guess are supposed to be genuine, but seem as scripted as professional wrestling.

American's Got Talent and *American Idol* exemplify American nationalism propaganda. These shows fill your TV screen with red, white, and blue stars (very often upside down) and stripes and reinforce the conditioning of American opportunity and freedom of choice. You get to call or text in and vote your favorite act of dozens through. However, when it comes time to voting for President of the United States you get two choices: dumb or dumber.

People who notice things are given *some* respite in the mainstream media, but in the guise of humor. In his later years George Carlin had spoken out candidly on mainstream television interviews and celebrity panels about the looting in America of the masses by the world's wealthiest, about America being on its last leg, about how the media deceives and the government lies, and about how our freedom is an illusion. John Stewart similarly will call some shit out. So when truths of our situation are allowed to surface, they affect not the frontal lobes but the funny bone. The conditioning gets more subtle in that it makes a lot of people who doubt the integrity of our media feel like there are still some people on 'their side' giving them a voice. Best off, it's not any of those crazy conspiracy theorists.

A Youtuber opened my eyes even more. It was his argument that Alex Jones is a reinvention of late controversial comedian Bill Hicks. The two are literally the same person, with Hicks having faked his death. Even with all the coincidences it seemed completely farfetched and highly unlikely for one reason: Bill Hicks was a comedic genius; Alex Jones isn't. Case closed. I indicated as much in a post of one of this tuber's tubes. He made a general statement back, chastising his small number of subscription members for their stupidity for not grasping the scope and enormity of this conspiracy. My feelings were hurt. A little. But it prompted me to open my eyes wider. And to reflect on a question I just assumed I had the answer to. Could the Illuminati infiltrate comedy?

Watching more of Bill Hicks' stand-up, I began to notice that what I considered genius was his insights, not as much his comedic talent (even though this appeared highly developed and original). His illumination made his comedic talent appear that much better. In addition, it's not far-reaching at all to infer that Mr. Hicks acts intentionally less funny now, as Jones. Alex Jones is often amusing and humorous…to perhaps the degree of say Regis Philbin…but he's several leagues below Hicks. Thus, I conclude, it is possible for the illuminati to infiltrate comedy. My automatic negation of this reality was brought on most likely by some sort of unidentified social conditioning.

Yet I think there is a limit to how far the Illuminati can infiltrate comedy. The Illuminati may be able to manufacture a Bill Hicks, possibly, but never a George Carlin. Carlin was one of the very few who had a voice anti-NWO that I'm convinced was 100% genuine. Sad loss. You know, he once indicated he thought he'd live a much longer life than how it turned out for him. He was revealing the Establishment more and more as old age settled in…in his stand-up and particularly talk show interviews. Youtube it. He tore paid detractors (the other guests and probably the host) down and humiliated them on television. He'd be finished saying something spot on and brilliant, and then he'd pull his hand out from under the table and in his palm were the testicles of the other guest. And he'd just hand them over to them. Awesome stuff.

Not withstanding a few current gems and geniuses, could the Illuminati be dumbing down the American sense of humor?

I get an uproarious delight watching Johnny Knoxville get his ass knocked cold by Butter Bean in a boxing match in the middle of a store. They woke Knoxville up and he said, "Is Butter Bean okay," before they took him to the hospital to have his head wound stitched.

There was a time when I probably would not have allowed myself to indulge in such frivolous humor (snob). Young kids will laugh at anything, I'd think. But, let's face it, funny is funny.

Bill Clinton's tongue is curled out above the corner of his upper lip while he works tirelessly to try to solve the pyd as he sits crossed legged on the sand, next to Papa Bush in his wheelchair. Dick Cheney piles the garbage bag half full of copies of The Great Flock of a New World Order onto the fire pit. The sky is maroon, and a little swirly.

"This all of them?" says Papa Bush.

"All but two," says Rumsfeld. "The Vatican has theirs, of course. And I got a haircut." He winks at Bush Sr.

"The Barber couldn't locate the third one?" says Papa Bush, incredulously.

"Guess not."

Papa Bush is quiet for several seconds. "He'll come through." He doesn't see Rummy roll his eyes.

Bush Jr. arrives, appearing hung-over. He plops down in a lawn chair, seeming nervous. Bush Sr. could never figure him out, and wonders how much truth about him was depicted by Jack Lutz in his controversial book. He pushes the thought out of his mind.

"Let's get the party started," he says, and feels himself loosening up a bit.

Cheney passes out pointed sticks and marshmallows. Rummy empties a can of lighter fluid on the pile of books. He lights a match, tosses it on the pile, and before the five of them is a raging fire. He and Papa Bush laugh as they watch the sinister bald eagle on the book covers melt.

"Bill, you solve that thing yet?" Bush Sr. says.

"Just about," he answers.

"Just about...."says Rummy."Hell, he doesn't even of the bottom layer matched."

"I can get it."

"Goddamn, give it to me, Bill." Papa Bush snatches the pyd out of his hands. He solves the pyramid puzzle, aligning all the correct colors in their respective layers, in less than twenty seconds. An eagle eye opens on his forehead, and he leans down and inserts the apex of the pyramid into its pupil. His head drops back, the pyramid still embedded, and out of his stretched jaws protrudes a screeching bird beak. His pants zipper opens, and four feathery tendrils spiral out of it, reaching far into the sky, swishing and whipping fiercely in circles. The atmosphere turns beet red, as shadowy figures take shape in the distance. George Jr. starts to panic, watching Bill, Rummy, and Dick strip to their white briefs and dance spastically in circles about the fire, screeching in strange tongues. Their eyes are rolled to the back of their heads, revealing the whites. The shadowy figures slowly, seductively advance on hands and knees toward the party. Bush Jr. is repulsed by the emerging site of them--the She-Male Sex Beasts of Chaktachupa, evoked for a primitive all-night orgy. At least ten of them. The four demonic Presidents comprising the stone monument in the distance start crooning, barbershop quartet style, the 1980's Billy Joel classic "For The Longest Time."

Bush Jr. clumsily falls over in his lawn chair and shuffle-runs in the direction of the house, sweating profusely, heart thumping.

Behind him, Papa Bush looks at him, and screams from his bald eagle head: "Junior!"

Bush Jr. scrambles down the hill in the brush, tripping on a root and tumbling the rest the way. He reaches the two-story farm house. Inside he sprints past his mom and Laura, both watching a rerun of Hee Haw on the television. He hears his mom say, "Is everything ok?" and then he locks himself in the bathroom. Panting and trembling, he pulls a worn copy of The Great Flock of a New World Order from inside the front of his slacks and opens it to where it's dog-eared. Clenching the book in one hand, he unzips his throbbing fly and begins reading aloud: "George Jr. packs his suitcase on his bed...."

Boardgames

We experience NWO propaganda not only in the form of audio/visual media programming, but in other popular pastimes. For instance: boardgames. Do you believe iconic games such as *Monopoly* and *Life* were created for mere family fun night entertainment? They are used, one, as a tool of distraction and pacifism, but they also indoctrinate the players. In Monopoly, we're taught the value of capitalism and cut-throat competition, and that building a monopoly and bankrupting the poor is a virtue.

We learn this hands-on. In simulation. It primes us for the big simulation later. You get to role-play a ruthless money grubbing capitalist. Thus very early in life we experience the head rush of accumulating wealth and power at the expense of all other people. If we play once a week then we're on a reinforcement schedule. You further practice the ritual with people you love and care for....priming you for future detachment from loved ones. Hey, it's the name of the game! If you're playing against your parents you get the added experience of toppling authority…provided you play by the rules.

Payday was always enjoyable as a kid. You get to pay bills, invest money, and borrow cash from the bank to pay your bills if you don't have enough. Wow, being an adult must be really fun.

Just as in 'real life' (i.e., Pop Illuminati), you don't start with paper currency of your own. You get it from the bank. Fortunately at the beginning of the game the $3,500 dollars the bank gives you to start with does not have to be repaid. Not so in the game of Pop Illuminati. In Pop Illuminati all players are expected to repay that money at interest. But how can all four players at the table pay the bank back 14,000 (4 x 3,500) *plus interest?* After all four players pay back their 3,500, there is no more money in the game play. It's all been returned to the bank.

We can see why in boardgames the banks don't charge interest on the money it gives the players to start out with. It would be absurd...the game would not work right. You, your boyfriend, your sister, and her girlfriend would all be sitting around the kitchen table with your drinks and popcorn, handing each other the instruction pamphlet all with dumbfounded looks on your face. Because all four of you are wise enough to know that *you can't pay back what does not exist.*

We can see the absurdity of this in the context of a boardgame played with four players, but in a game like Pop Illuminati with billions of players, it's not easy to see, so everyone continues to play the absurd game.

"He who has the gold sets the rules."
~The Golden Rule according to *They Live*

You and the U.S. government are in debt to the Federal Reserve--a conglomerate of private banks never audited by our government or any of us. 'Federal' is misleading in that there is nothing federal about them. 'The Federal Reserve is as federal as the Federal Express,' it's often said. They are not government run and operate independently. They adjust the nation's credit and create money from thin air and inject it into the system--Pop Illuminati--at their whim, like they're ancient Greek gods or some shit. In fact they created all the U.S. Currency in circulation out of thin air. Whenever they inject the new fake currency into the system--this fiat or phony *Payday* money--prices go up. Inflation. But they don't go up right away. No, the rich get the phony money first and purchase things at the current price. By the time any of this loaned fake money reaches the lower classes the prices of things have already shot up, so that the increased money really does not even pay the difference of the increased price. The rich get richer, the world bankers get more powerful, and you and I get by on less and less.

This is a crude explanation. I'm not an economist, of course, but it really does not take an economist to understand this. For a more detailed explanation on how the banking system operates and robs us, I suggest the following books:

The Creature from Jekyll Island: A Second Look at the Federal Reserve. 5th edition. G. Edward Griffin. American Media. 2010.

They Own it All (Including You!): By Means of Toxic Currency. Ronald MacDonald, Robert Rowen. Book Surge Publishing. 2009.

The Trillion-Dollar Conspiracy: How The New World Order, Man-Made Diseases, and Zombie Banks Are Destroying America. Jim Marrs. William Morrow Paperbacks. Reprint edition. 2011.

The middle portion of the documentary *Zeitgeist* provides an awesome visual depiction of our banking system (the rest of the film is New World Order propaganda, especially the last part on The Venus Project). There is also an excellent, informative and very entertaining short cartoon film by The Provocateur Network.

The old 70s or 80s version of *Payday* is still out in my dad's garage. I acquired a newer version several years ago. I've periodically played the game over the years with my nephew. Rereading the instructions recently, I instantly recognized the NWO propaganda.

Do you?:

"*As any financial advisor will tell you, the way to get ahead is to take risks and [invest]....The time will probably come, however, when you don't have enough money on hand [to invest] or pay your bills, pay a neighbor, or make a charitable donation. Do what all investers have had to do from time-to-time: Take out a LOAN!*" (from *Payday* instruction booklet; Hasbro; 2000)

Several versions of the Illuminati card game have been put out over the last several years. According to legend, the creator, Steve Jackson, nearly didn't get the game out. Supposedly the Illuminati failed in their attempt to thwart the game's release (as if they'd ever failed at anything...) The cool cartoon depictions of various NWO conspiracy phenomena are very interesting. Some of the cards seem to foretell the 911 catastrophes. On the games website, one card, called the Terrorist Nuke, released in 1995, depicts two Twin Towers, one exploding at about the same position that the airplane hit on 911. Another card, released the same year, shows an explosion at the center of the pentagon. Notice how the smoke trails over the side, obscuring it and bringing to mind the 'plane' that 'crashed' into the side of the Pentagon.

Under the gaze of the harvest moon, I cruise down the street, stoned and smoking a square, looking at all the deserted and decrepit buildings. 3am. The multi-shaded dark purple sky rolls, swirls, and twists. It's quiet, chilly. Jimi Hendrix croons about a Purple Haze on my radio. Six days to go to turn in the first draft of my manuscript....Been up three days. Gotta make my car payment. Can't lose it. Need to clean out the toilet. Need...water turned back on. Need my meds. Fuck the meds. Gotta stop payment to those assholes to pay these assholes. Stiff those assholes this month.

I pull up to the red light. Cop behind me. I hope she does not get offended by the Ron Paul sticker. Are they profiling for this in our meager city yet? Am I domestic terrorist suspect? If she pulls me over, what will happen when she discovers the car is not covered? Hope I don't have another tail light out. Who can afford such shit. Where's my cigarette cherry? Fuck! My nuts!

Mountain Dew makes for miserable ballsack.

I look up at the large sun above me. Mocking. Well I suppose a Day's Hotel *should have a rising sun logo on their sign.*

Green means go. At the next intersection I stop and look up at the sun. I leave a little room for the truck pulling out of the BP *gas station to get out, and sigh.*

The cop has pulled next to me now. In mirrored sunglasses. She grins, showing me her tooth, decaying. I wince-grin and then stare off at the black and white checkered flag on the Advance AutoParts *logo across the street and wonder about the origin of the checkered flag in auto racing and am sure the Freemasons had a cloven foot in it. It waves.*

I look over at the cop. The light changes in her eye.

Green is go. We peel out. I amp up the stereo—ZZ Top crunching out my speakers like tres loco shoddily shaded Pac-Men *loaded on tequila. Reaching into the side pocket of my*

brown leather blazer, I pull out a box of Marlboros, *flip open
the apex of the pyramid, tongue out a twig and light up.*
    Three tail lights rattle away rapidly.

The Digital MegaBrain

"I'm an analog man in a digital world, gonna find me an analog girl."
~**Joe Walsh, "Analog Man" from the album** *Analog Man* **(2012)**

Facebook is one but many data collection tools the Illuminati uses on you for your personal file (they have one on each of us). Think about all the transactions and behaviors you engage in that leave a digital record of some sort. It's all compiled, sorted, organized, and run through specialized statistical application software comparing it with other people's information—finding trends, correlations, opportunities, risks, threats, and so on. Perhaps their software will one day soon become so sophisticated as to detect crimes before they happen – like in Philip K. Dick's *Minority Report* (film starring Tom Cruise).

It dumbs down our language….LOL, BRB, ROFL, LMFAO, etc...paralleling Orwell's Newspeak in *1984*. (If you are at this point mentally objecting, saying, "wait, the Illuminati didn't invent facebook. Mark Zuckerberg did. Everybody knows that," that is okay. How do you know that everybody knows it?) It's such an effective data collection tool because it is ubiquitous and also people *want* to provide the information. And it's cheap to run. Those NWO bastards jumped all over this idea. Of course, the vast majority of people are ignorant in what they are actually doing when volunteering their personal information. And I'm not just alluding to simple demographic information—such as gender, age, city, job, university attended, marriage status, favorite sexual position, etc. Or even all of your interests, the movies, music, and books you like, doggy style, and so forth. You tell about what you did that day and how you felt about it and how so-and-so responded. You share your aspirations, dreams, and reveal your weaknesses. In fact, you reveal information about yourself on a daily basis every time you post *anything at all.*

It might be you like it on top. But my point is that any post that you make, from a single period to several paragraphs, tells something about you.

"Here Comes the Sun..."
~The Beatles, from the album *Abbey Road* (1969)

Facebook can in one sense be compared to a personal diary that the 'world' reads. It's ingenious in that posters are instantly reinforced via sharing their thoughts and feelings, by way of attention, consolation, feedback, etc. Facebook even prompts users to post what is on their mind. On your wall, it says something like: "What's on your mind?" Facebook for many becomes an addiction. How brilliant is that? The Illuminati has engineered a way for you to actually fiend to provide them your personal information.

The Illuminati's advanced computer software will detect 'red flags' of people who they might deem as domestic terrorists (e.g., conspiracy theorists), so it's not as if a person in a white lab coat has to monitor your behavior directly all of the time. Furthermore, all of your Facebook friends and you have unwittingly been recruited as NWO "thought police" (read George Orwell's *1984*). They watch you and keep you in line via social pressure to conform. When you expand your Facebook friends list to include almost every acquaintance you know, do you see the continual surveillance of your personal life, to which this expansion leads? Now, your coworkers, family, friends, neighbors see nearly everything. They collectively and functionally become the all-seeing-eye.

Our intrusiveness is on continuous increase as new 'convenient' features are added to Facebook regularly. We can now see via a convenient scrawl to the right of the screen what everybody's up to. Whose post they 'liked.' Whose picture they 'liked' (e.g., "Bitch. I saw you like his pic! You never like anybody else's pic!"). Etc. Furthermore, our police force is equipped with the new capability to know when the other user we are having a private discussion with sees our latest response (e.g., "WTF, man? I know u there. I know u see because it say u see."). We've become the Gestapo.

Kundilini.

Technology advances so rapidly that it's hard to see what we as a society are turning into as Facebook becomes a central focus in our lives. Certainly, it's another double-edged sword, which is a reason it is so effective: we get to connect with friends and family we never see, and we get to build up a profile for instant ego inflation.

Sometimes you might get an uncomfortable sense: who are these Facebook friends I share facets of my personal self to daily? Some I've never met in person, and some I know really well, but have not seen in years. Do these people even exist other than in megabytes and pixels and as constructs in my mind? Are we becoming so cut-off and complacent as a people that we would just as soon 'know' these people through digital and computerized means? If so, what does it tell us about our evolution as a society?

Not only is Facebook an ingenious psychological assessment tool, it is an equally ingenious sociological assessment tool. It creates the experimental condition of a simulated society--a micro-society that reflects our real society that the social scientists can look over and directly observe. It's a sociologist's wet dream. And it is even better than say if they could just have a bird's eye view of people's interactions and observable behavior in every day life, because it allows for the psychological peek inside the minds of the individual subjects. A social psychologist's wet dream.

Kundilini...

And then when a significant political or social event is 'reported' by our mainstream media--for instance, 'info' on a school shooting or the signing into law a new 'Executive Order' on gun control by the President--the mad NWO social scientists drool as they examine the effects these media reported events have on the population.

Of course, there is a segment of the population that does not yet use Facebook. It cannot be assumed the Facebook micro-society is representative of the population at large. The Illuminati's got it covered. We can be certain that Facebook is merely a facet of Phase One of what we'll just call the Illuminati Digital Megabrain Project. The IDMP works toward the total integration of human mental life.

Kundilini.

Two horned snakes--one black, one white--wriggle and slither, twisting, curling around the spiked feet, and up. They squirm, crisscrossing, coiling, ascending. Rubbing, hissing, and moaning. Across Christ's johnson, and upward. Turning, bending, intersecting, winding. A writhing helix. They stop and gaze at one another over the crown of thorns. The black one winks at the white one.

They dart through either of Christ's ears, devouring, tunneling through gray flesh. Their forked tongues meet at the pineal gland. The black one bites it, and both reptiles fuse like a Twizzler *and slither into the gland.*

Christ opens his bright, green reptilian eyes. Gazing upon the live sheep scattered below, he licks his chops, noticing the emergence of long sharp fangs. He grins and his earlobes grow to points. His torso turns scaly with patches of coarse black fur. Gray spiral horns curl from his temples. His muscle mass doubles, and he rips his hands from the cross. They enlarge and turn to furry scaly claws before his fascinated eyes. The cacophony of baas burns his brain and sets his crown of thorns ablaze.

From nowhere kicks in Johnny Cash's Ring of Fire.

Christ grips the horizontal board for leverage and tears his feet from the third spike. Leaping from the cross he begins a massacre of unbiblical proportions. Pouncing with the agility of a cheetah from one shrieking lamb to the next, he bites through throats. Clawing, ripping out hearts and swallowing them whole within a blizzard of wool.

The Cash song ends when the last lamb cries out, and from within the silence Jesus hears the start of a primitive drum beat. Miles away, ascending from the skyline, an enormous sun. A thousand feminine arms jut out from behind the radiant, yellow disk. The bejeweled arms rhythmically sway in sync, along with the beat.

The Son of Man sucks raw veal from his teeth and grins. He laughs maniacally. He howls and a torrent of tears blends with the blood on his face. Sprinting on all fours in the direction of the sun, within a few minutes...

....leaping and disappearing through the center of it.

The bejeweled arms all stretch and stiffen, palms opened, fingers spread, hands waving side to side--the sound of a crashing tambourine--

And the sun sets in the gray sky.

COMING SOON!!
The drinking game resumes.
Wrap your brain around...
Pop Illuminati Volume II: The Cosmic Yin Yang Holomind
Let the meeting of the Holominds begin!
In Holovision
A Randy Cunningham Pyd

ABOUT THE AUTHOR

Randy Cunningham is a former mental health professional gone mad. When he's not attempting to scare the bejeezus out of Facebook friends with lurid conspiracy theories concerning the Illuminati's impending New World Order and global depopulation agenda, he's reading, writing, brooding, raising his miniature poodle, and trying to find work of any sort.

His first book, the controversial conspiracy chiller **The Great Flock of a New World Order**, was published under the pseudonym Jack Lutz in 2011. It will be available under his real name as a limited edition chapbook containing several extras through Dynatox Ministries. Upcoming releases include **Order Conspiracy Theory and Popular Culture**; and **Pop Illuminati Volume II: The Cosmic Yin Yang Holomind**. They are destined to be his magnum opus and claim to intergalactic fame--according to him.

Randy Cunningham hones a lasting erotic love for each and every reader of his works.